Bible
Trivia
?? for Kids

Fun
Bible
Trivia
?? for Kids
?

More Than 700
Knowledge-Testing,
Brain-Bending,
HEAD-SCRATCHING
Questions for Kids Ages 8-12

BARBOUR
PUBLISHING

Published by Barbour Publishing, Inc., P.O. Box 719, Uhrichsville, Ohio 44683 www.barbourbooks.com

Our mission is to publish and distribute inspirational products offering exceptional value and biblical encouragement to the masses.

 Member of the
Evangelical Christian
Publishers Association

Printed in the United States of America.
Offset Paperback Manufacturers, Dallas, PA 18612; January 2014; D10004302

CONTENTS

SO YOU THINK YOU KNOW YOUR BIBLE?

Find out just how smart you are with this book! Written especially for eight- to twelve-year-olds, *Fun Bible Trivia for Kids* is challenging, humorous, true to the Scriptures. . .and just plain fun!

Multiple choice, true/false, and open-ended questions will test your knowledge of the Old and New Testaments. . .from Noah's long sea cruise, to the Ten Commandments, to bread in the Bible, to the birth of Jesus, to a lady named Martha. . . whew, you name it.

Find out just how well you know God's Word with *Fun Bible Trivia for Kids*! Answers begin on page 189.

1. THE OLD TESTAMENT

1. True or false: Most of the Old Testament was originally written in the Hebrew language.

2. True or false: The Old Testament was written before Christ was born.

3. The first five books of the Bible are called the:

   a) Pentateuch
   b) Pentagon
   c) Pimiento
   d) Fantastic Five

4. Who wrote the first five books of the Bible?

5. **Did you know the Jewish people call the first five books of the Bible the Torah? These books contain the Law given to Moses by God. Today many Jewish people follow dietary laws and other observances set forth in the Torah. Jesus said Christians do not need to follow these laws (John 1:17). However, we worship the same God, Jehovah, and Christians are to follow the Ten Commandments.**

6. **You can find the Ten Commandments in the following Old Testament book(s):**

      a) Exodus

      b) Deuteronomy

      c) Exodus and Deuteronomy

      d) Genesis

7. **Can you name all of the Ten Commandments?**

8. The first event in the Old Testament is the:

   a) creation of the universe

   b) creation of the first gospel singing group

   c) great flood

   d) birth of Jesus

9. In the Old Testament, the nation of Israel was divided into how many tribes?

10. What are the names of the twelve tribes of Israel?

11. The Law in the Pentateuch is often called the Mosaic Law because:

   a) God gave the laws to Moses

   b) all the laws are different, creating a "mosaic" of instructions

   c) Moses broke the stone tablets and made up his own law

   d) Moses was a police officer

12. Why do you think there are so many names listed in several of the early Old Testament books?

13. The Book of Ruth:

    a) is named for the candy bar, Baby Ruth

    b) records great military victories

    c) is the story of an evil woman named Ruth

    d) illustrates two kinds of love

14. Esther:

    a) held a triathlon to see who would be her king

    b) won a beauty contest and married the king

    c) paid the king a lot of money to marry her because she was ugly

    d) was not Jewish

15. True or false: Queen Esther is honored by Jewish people today.

16. The book of Job relates how:

    a) to get a good job

    b) God protects and rewards those who love Him

    c) to cover up those ugly sores

    d) friends help out when the going gets tough

17. True or false: King David, who wrote many of the Psalms, was the father of King Solomon, who wrote Ecclesiastes and most of Proverbs.

18. A psalter:

    a) sprinkles salt

    b) mines salt

    c) makes a habit of asking, "Would you please pass the salt?"

    d) sings praises to God

19. Did you know the word *psalm* means religious song? The book of Psalms is a collection of worshipful songs praising the Lord. Although David wrote many of them, others contributed to this book as well. Psalms from this book are often used in church worship services. You might also use them as prayers when you talk to God by yourself. Take a look at the book of Psalms. See if you can find one that speaks to you today.

20. Anyone looking for wisdom from King Solomon can consult:

    a) *Sports Illustrated*
    b) John
    c) Proverbs
    d) Psalms

21. True or false: King Solomon also wrote the book of Lamentations.

22. Ecclesiastes teaches us that:

    a) earth's glories fade, but God is forever
    b) Solomon should have picked an easier title to spell than Ecclesiastes
    c) Solomon had very little money
    d) Solomon had trouble in school

23. True or false: We know who wrote all of the books of the Old Testament.

24. Pretend you are a Bible scholar trying to find out when the events of a certain book of the Bible took place. What would you look for?

25. A prophet is:

    a) an astronomer

    b) a psychic

    c) one who interprets dreams

    d) one sent by God to tell His plans
       for the future

26. A true prophet:

    a) always has good news

    b) is not always sent from God

    c) works for profit

    d) often is sent to warn God's people to
       repent of sin

2. THE CRUISE OF A LIFETIME

1. You can find the story of Noah's ark in the book of

    a) Genesis

    b) Revelation

    c) The Love Boat

    d) Noah

2. True or false: In Noah's time, God was pleased with his creation.

3. In Noah's time, God decided He would

    a) rain manna on all the people

    b) destroy all the people, animals, and birds he had created

    c) give everyone a computer for school

    d) send missionaries to give everyone a New Testament Bible

4. True or false: Noah was the only good man living in his time.

5. How many sons did Noah have?

6. Can you name Noah's sons? Hint: One of them has the same name as a famous Virginia meat product.

7. Did you know that God told Noah to take seven pairs of each type of bird with him into the ark (Genesis 7:3)? He also told Noah to take one pair of each ritually unclean animal and seven pairs of each ritually clean animal (Genesis 7:2).

8. What is a ritually clean beast?

9. When the flood started Noah was

- a) 6 years old
- b) 60 years old.
- c) 600 years old
- d) 666 years old

10. How long did it rain?

11. Did you know that the water rose until it was about twenty-five feet over the highest mountains? (See Genesis 7:20.)

12. Noah could see the mountaintops after

    a) 7½ months

    b) 10 months

    c) 7 days

    d) 40 days and 40 nights

13. Did you know that, after the flood, the water did not start going down for 150 days?

14. True or false: The first bird Noah sent out from the ark was a dove.

15. After the second time out, the dove brought Noah

    a) a Rebecca St. James CD

    b) another dove

    c) a McDonald's Happy Meal

    d) an olive branch

16. True or false: Noah was 601 years old when he and his family got out of the ark.

17. After God saved Noah's family from the flood, Noah

      a) opened Noah's Yacht Club

      b) made a golden calf

      c) built an altar to God and made sacrifices upon it

      d) learned to swim

18. True or false: God promised not to destroy the earth by flood again.

19. What caused God to make such a promise?

20. What do we often see after rainfall that reminds us of God's promise to Noah?

19

3. A TOWERING PROBLEM

1. **Where in the Bible can you find the story of the Tower of Babel?**

2. **True or false: When the people first started building the Tower of Babel, they all spoke the same language.**

3. **The people who built the tower spoke**
   a) Latin
   b) Hebrew
   c) Klingon
   d) an unspecified language

4. **The tower was built of**
   a) wood
   b) stone
   c) brick
   d) steel

5. **True or false: The people were building a city as well as a tower.**

6. The people wanted a tower that would

a) let them see the Atlantic Ocean

b) be three feet taller than the Empire State Building

c) make a suitable home for Rapunzel

d) reach to heaven

7. True or false: God was happy when He saw the tower.

8. When He saw the tower, God

a) gave the people a golden calf

b) asked Satan to loan the builders pitchforks to help them finish it

c) told the workmen how to make better bricks

d) made the people all speak different languages so they couldn't finish the work

9. Why is the story of the Tower of Babel important?

4. GOD'S PROMISE TO ABRAHAM

1. True or false: The story of Abraham is found in the book of Genesis.

2. In which chapter can you find the story of God's promise to Abraham?

3. True or false: Abraham was named Abram before God changed his name.

4. How old was Abraham when God appeared to him?

5. God told Abraham to

   a) build an ark

   b) become Jesus' disciple

   c) obey Him

   d) make a movie called *The Ten Commandments*

6. When Abraham saw God, he

    a) told God he was afraid

    b) bowed down, touching his face to the ground

    c) built an altar

    d) asked Him for a son

7. God wanted to make a covenant with Abraham. What is a covenant?

8. True or false: God promised Abraham he would have many descendants.

9. A descendant is

    a) a relative of a future generation

    b) an ancestor

    c) a person walking down a staircase

    d) an airplane going down in the sky

10. God also promised Abraham

    a) great riches

    b) a chariot and seven swift horses

    c) a coat of many colors

    d) the land of Canaan

11. True or false: God plans for His covenant with Abraham to last forever.

12. God gave Abram the name Abraham because

    a) it fit better with the song "Father Abraham"

    b) it was easier to spell

    c) Abraham was to be the father of many nations

    d) He wanted to name him after Abraham Lincoln

13. True or false: God said that some of Abraham's descendants would be kings.

14. True or false: As part of the covenant, God wanted Abraham and his descendants to worship Him.

24

15. God changed the name of Abraham's wife. Do you remember what Sarah's name was before God changed it?

16. God promised Sarah she would

      a) never have to work again

      b) live in a tent until she was ninety

      c) have a baby

      d) be the first woman president of the United States

17. When God promised Abraham that his wife, Sarah, would have a baby, Abraham

      a) bowed down to God

      b) laughed

      c) sang God a psalm

      d) wrote the Pentateuch

18. Which did God promise Sarah, a baby boy, or a baby girl?

19. Abraham was surprised by God's promise because Sarah

> a) had vowed never to have children
>
> b) was CEO of a large company and had no time for kids
>
> c) was ninety years old, which is usually too old to have a baby
>
> d) already had thirteen boys

20. How old was Abraham when God promised him that Sarah would bear a baby?

21. An heir is

a) a person with too much hair

b) an honest mistake

c) a person who receives an inheritance

d) an airhead

22. True or false: God agreed with Abraham that Ishmael should be Abraham's heir.

5. THE TEN COMMANDMENTS

1. Did you know that the Ten Commandments appear in the Bible twice? You can find them in Exodus 20:1–17 and Deuteronomy 5:1–21.

2. True or false: Exodus and Deuteronomy are both New Testament books.

3. Who wrote the first five books of the Bible?

4. Did you know that the first five books of the Bible are called the Pentateuch?

5. Can you name all five books of the Pentateuch?

6. When God issued the Ten Commandments, He was on

    a) the banks of the River Jordan

    b) Mount Sinai

    c) Israel's TV Channel 6

    d) Mount Ararat

7. Did you know that Exodus means departure?

8. When God gave them the Ten Commandments, the Israelites had just

    a) traveled the Information Highway

    b) been brought out of slavery in Egypt

    c) discovered electricity

    d) celebrated the release of the movie *Star Wars*

9. True or false: The first commandment is God's law to worship no other god except Him.

10. Do you think The first commandment is the most important? Why?

11. **True or false:** It is okay to worship statues, money, and other earthly goods as long as we attend church every Sunday.

12. **What does God mean when He says not to take His name "in vain"?**

13. **God commands us to set aside one day a week to**

    a) gather manna
    b) read the Bible and only drink water all day
    c) watch cartoons
    d) keep holy, cease work, and remember His people's deliverance from Egypt

14. **True or false:** On the Sabbath, the head of the household may rest, but everyone else should work.

15. Why did God say He wanted us to rest every seventh day?

16. Think about the Sabbath. How do you show your love to God on His special day?

17. God tells us to honor our

    a) pastor

    b) friends

    c) father and mother

    d) teachers and principal

18. True or false: The sixth commandment tells us not to murder.

19. God's commandment not to commit adultery shows us how much God values marriage. Where does God establish the institution of marriage?

20. The eighth commandment tells us not to

    a) burp in public

    b) be mean to our brothers and sisters

    c) steal

    d) be angry with others

21. The King James Version of the Bible tells us that God says not to "bear false witness" against our neighbor. The New International Version says we should not give "false testimony." What do these phrases in Exodus 20:16 and Deuteronomy 5:20 mean?

22. Sometimes it is hard not to lie because the truth can hurt someone's feelings. How can you be truthful without being mean?

23. God tells us not to covet other people's possessions. That means we should not

    a) steal from our friends

    b) destroy other people's belongings

    c) make fun of others

    d) wish we had our neighbor's stuff

24. God also gave Moses other laws. Most of them can be found in the book of

    a) Leviticus

    b) Numbers

    c) Acts

    d) Revelation

25. The Lord wrote the Ten Commandments on

    a) sheepskin

    b) stone tablets

    c) parchment

    d) Thursday

26. True or false: The original copy of the Ten Commandments is on display at the Jerusalem Museum.

27. Now that you have learned about the Ten Commandments, can you name all of them?

6. JOSHUA'S FAMOUS BATTLE

1. Did you know that when he was a young man, Joshua served in the tabernacle? (Exodus 33:11).

2. True or false: Moses was led by God to appoint Joshua to be his successor.

3. The book of Joshua begins recording what happened right after

    a) the Israelites went whitewater rafting on the Jordan River

    b) the American Revolution

    c) the death of Moses

    d) the birth of Jesus

4. Is Joshua found in the Old Testament or the New Testament?

5. Who wrote the book of Joshua?

6. God told Joshua to take the people of Israel to the land He had promised them, located across the

    a) Red Sea

    b) Grand Canyon

    c) Jordan River

    d) Nile River

7. True or false: God said the Israelites should never become discouraged because He would be with them where ever they went.

8. Joshua's spies in Jericho stayed at

    a) a Holiday Inn

    b) a Pharisee's house

    c) the home of a wicked woman

    d) Mary Magdalene's house

9. True or false: Rahab protected the spies from the men of Jericho.

10. Did you know that no one could leave or enter a city after the gate was closed at sundown? Rahab tricked the men who were chasing Joshua's spies and told them to look outside the city. Because the men were locked out after sundown, they could not harm the spies (Joshua 2:4–7).

11. Rahab hid the spies

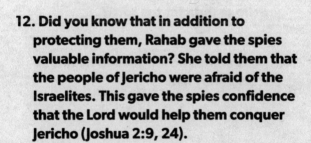

   a) on the roof
   b) in the wine cellar
   c) in the bathtub
   d) under her bed

12. Did you know that in addition to protecting them, Rahab gave the spies valuable information? She told them that the people of Jericho were afraid of the Israelites. This gave the spies confidence that the Lord would help them conquer Jericho (Joshua 2:9, 24).

13. True or false: Rahab accepted the Lord and asked the spies for mercy.

14. Why did Rahab protect the spies?

15. Did you know that God stopped the Jordan River from flowing while the Israelites crossed it into the promised land? The river was usually flooded at that time of year, so crossing it on foot would have been impossible without God's miracle. The stopping of the river also allowed the ark of the covenant to stay dry while the priests carried it (Joshua 3:14–17).

16. What was the ark of the covenant?

17. How many men crossed the plains of Jericho to fight for the Lord?

18. The Israelites no longer had manna to eat after they had

    a) been punished for watching too much TV

    b) eaten food grown in the promised land

    c) gotten tired of eating quail meat

    d) sinned

19. What was manna?

20. True or false: The walls of Jericho came tumbling down after the Israelites threw rocks and stones at them.

21. Whose family was spared during the fall of Jericho?

22. All the silver, gold, bronze, and iron in Jericho was

    a) used to improve the ark of the covenant

    b) put into the Lord's treasury

    c) used to build the Tower of Babel

    d) made into fancy jewelry

23. True or False: After the fall of Jericho, Joshua became famous in the land.

7. NOT EXACTLY JUDGE JUDY

1. Where in the Old Testament can we find
   out about the judges of Israel?

2. Did you know the name Deborah means
   "hornet"?

3. True or false: Female judges were
   common in the Old Testament.

4. Deborah was also a:
   - a) clerk at a video store
   - b) soccer player
   - c) computer programmer
   - d) prophet

5. True or false: In Deborah's time, Israel
   was a free nation.

6. King Jabin of Canaan:

    a) made life very hard for the Israelites

    b) promised to get rid of baseball trading cards

    c) forced the Israelites to worship gold statues of himself

    d) served pepperoni pizza in school cafeterias every Friday

7. How many iron chariots did King Jabin have?

8. How many years did the Israelites live under King Jabin's rule before they asked God for help?

9. Why was God punishing Israel at this time?

10. True or false: After the people cried out for help, the Lord told Deborah what to do to deliver her people.

11. Deborah planned to:

- a) poison the enemy's water supply
- b) pray for a plague of frogs to torture the enemy
- c) deliver the enemy into the hands of Israel's general
- d) ask the general to use stealth fighter planes to bomb the enemy

12. The enemy was to be defeated at Mount Tabor. Where was Mount Tabor located?

13. Barak was:

- a) awarded a Purple Heart medal for bravery
- b) the inventor of the nuclear submarine
- c) a general in Israel's army
- d) Deborah's husband

14. Rather than confront the enemy alone, Barak wanted to take along:

- a) Deborah, to ensure success
- b) his hand-held video game in case he got bored
- c) his lucky rabbit's foot
- d) 10,000 men, to outnumber the king's army

15. Deborah agreed but said the credit for the victory would go to:

a) Barak

b) a woman

c) McDonald's, for providing the army with hamburgers

d) Pepsi, Reebok, and Tide, the army's corporate sponsors

16. True or false: In Old Testament times, it was customary for women in Israel to lead battles because in that nation, they were considered superior to men.

17. Did God give the Israelites complete victory over Sisera's army?

18. You can read a poem about the battle in:

a) the fifth chapter of Judges

b) the first chapter of Genesis

c) *The Butter Battle Book* by Dr. Seuss

d) the book of Revelation

19. After the people of Israel cried out to God for help, He answered their prayers. When was the last time you prayed to God for help? What happened?

8. MEET ELIJAH

1. We first meet Elijah in:

    a) 1 Kings

    b) Genesis

    c) Acts

    d) his swimming trunks

2. Elijah was:

    a) a doctor

    b) an actor playing the role of a doctor

    c) a prophet

    d) the writer of the Gospel of John

3. True or false: Elijah served the Lord of Israel.

4. Elijah told King Ahab there would be:

    a) great profits from his new racetrack

    b) seven years of bounty, followed by seven years of famine

    c) a great ship named *Titanic* that would sink on her maiden voyage

    d) no rain for the next few years until God commanded rain to fall

5. Why do you think God told Elijah to give King Ahab this message?

6. True or false: King Ahab was a godly king who loved the Lord.

7. King Ahab:

   a) honored the God of Israel with sacrifices pleasing to Him

   b) worshipped the god Baal

   c) went on television to proclaim God's greatness

   d) was the best king Israel ever had

8. God told Elijah to hide by Kerith Ravine (1 Kings 17:2–3). A ravine is a gorge or gap in the land. The King James Version of the Bible calls this location brook Cherith. We can assume from this that brook Cherith was located in Kerith Ravine.

9. Kerith Ravine was located:

   a) east of Eden

   b) west of Jordan

   c) east of Jordan

   d) near one of Michael Jordan's homes

10. God told Elijah to hide because:

   a) Elijah's prophecy had made King Ahab mad

   b) he was famous and God wanted him to avoid photographers

   c) King Ahab wanted to honor him with food forbidden to Jews

   d) hide-and-seek was the favorite game of King Ahab's small son

11. While he was hiding, Elijah's food would be brought to him by:

   a) ravens

   b) doves

   c) pretty maids all in a row

   d) an ice cream truck, since the ravine was on its route

12. Look at your answer to the last question. Why would they bring Elijah his food?

44

13. Elijah's food consisted of:

    a) bagels and lox in the morning and matzo ball soup in the evening

    b) eggs and bacon in the morning and a ham and cheese sandwich in the evening

    c) any food his heart desired

    d) bread and meat in the morning and evening

14. After the brook dried up, Elijah was fed by:

    a) bigger, better ravens

    b) a widow

    c) locusts

    d) John the Baptist

15. Why did the brook dry up?

16. True or false: The widow who fed Elijah after the brook dried up had plenty of rich food to eat.

45

17. After the widow's son died, Elijah:

> a) told her she shouldn't have let him hang out on the street corner
> b) gave her herbs and green tea
> c) said she should have called 911 sooner
> d) prayed to God

18. True or false: The widow's son rose from the dead.

19. Some people said Jesus was:

> a) Elijah
> b) John the Baptist
> c) Jeremiah
> d) all of the above

20. True or false: Jesus spoke to Moses and Elijah before He was crucified.

21. Why would the Jews be looking for Elijah to come back from the dead?

22. True or false: Jesus said Elijah had returned.

9. ELISHA PERFORMS MANY MIRACLES

1. True or false: Elisha was the son of the prophet Elijah.

2. You can find out about Elisha in
    a) 1 Kings
    b) 2 Kings
    c) Matthew
    d) Revelation

3. Did you know that Elijah was taken to heaven by a chariot of fire (2 Kings 2:11)?

4. Can you name another godly person who was taken to heaven without dying?

5. True or false: Elisha asked for a "double portion" of Elijah's spirit.

6. Elisha's first miracle was

    a) making 5,000 sandwiches from one can of Spam

    b) dividing the Jordan River and walking on dry land

    c) inventing the cotton gin

    d) getting the children of Jericho to eat broccoli soup

7. True or false: The fifty prophets of Jericho saw the miracle and proclaimed that Elijah's power was upon Elisha.

8. In Jericho, Elisha

    a) opened a Coca-Cola factory

    b) gave a bowl of broccoli soup to every child he met

    c) made the water pure

    d) turned water into wine

9. Some boys in Bethel made fun of Elisha for being

    a) a stamp collector

    b) vertically challenged

    c) bald

    d) a dweeb

10. The Moabites had

    a) poisoned the Jordan River

    b) turned the Nile River red

    c) rebelled against Israel

    d) been involved in a junk bond scandal on Wall Street

11. True or false: Elisha told the kings to build ditches in a dry stream bed.

12. The next day, the Moabites decided to loot the Israelites' camp because

    a) Elisha told them to

    b) Jezebel rose from the dead and promised victory

    c) they thought the water they saw around the camp was blood

    d) they had promised to bring their girlfriends some jewelry

13. What happened when the Moabites reached the Israelites' camp?

14. True or false: The Israelites conquered all of Moab until only the capital city of Kir-haraseth was left.

15. Later a widow asked Elisha for help because she

    a) was in debt

    b) wanted to be beautiful

    c) wanted to find another husband

    d) wanted him to change the school cafeteria menu from fish sticks to pizza

16. The only item the widow had in her house was

     a) a small coin called a mite

     b) a brass monkey

     c) a picture of Jesus

     d) a small jar of olive oil

17. Describe the miracle that happened when the widow followed Elisha's instructions.

18. True or false: Because of Elisha's advice, the widow had enough money to pay off her debts, with enough left over to live on.

19. Elisha offered to put in a good word with the king for a rich woman who had been kind to him. Did she accept his offer?

20. Elisha rewarded the Shunammite woman's kindness by

    a) praising her to the king

    b) promising her that she would have a baby

    c) giving her permission to charge toll to people entering Jerusalem

    d) giving her free cable television for a year

21. The kindness that the woman had done for Elisha was

    a) giving him water at the well

    b) buying him tickets to see WrestleFest America

    c) setting up a room for him to stay in when he visited

    d) washing his feet with expensive CK One perfume

22. True or false: Years later, Elisha performed a miracle for the woman's son.

23. Elisha:

  a) brought the boy back from the dead

  b) refused to perform a miracle

  c) healed the boy's blindness

  d) gave the boy wisdom so he could pass his college entrance exams

24. Did you know that Elisha fed 100 men with twenty loaves of bread? Even though this normally would not have been enough food for so many, they all feasted and had food left over (2 Kings 4:42–44).

25. Which one of Jesus' miracles does this story make you remember?

26. True or false: Elisha purified a pot of stew that contained poisonous gourds.

27. True or false: Naaman was a respected Egyptian commander.

28. Naaman suffered from

   a) leprosy
   b) the flu
   c) negative cash flow
   d) cowardice

29. Who suggested that Elisha could cure Naaman?

30. When King Jehoram of Israel saw Naaman, he thought,

   a) "I'll be rich now!"
   b) "I will only ask for the silver, lest I look greedy."
   c) "I do not have the power of God! The Syrian king wants to quarrel with me."
   d) "Gross! A leper!"

31. True or false: Elisha was not afraid to try to heal Naaman. He told the king that he would prove Israel had a prophet.

32. Elisha sent his servant to tell Naaman to

    a) wash seven times in the Jordan River

    b) sacrifice five rams

    c) sit on a stump and say "Bobiddy Boo
       Boo!" three times

    d) go to a leper colony

**33. When Naaman was told what he should
do to get well, he**

    a) cried

    b) was angry

    c) was eager to proceed

    d) decided to kill Elisha

**34. True or false: Elisha's instructions
caused Naaman to become even sicker.**

**35. After Naaman was cured, whose god
did he vow to worship?**

36. The amount of soil Naaman took with him was

    a) a jar full
    b) a bushel
    c) a peck
    d) two mule loads

37. Did you know Elisha refused to accept any payment in return for curing Naaman? (See 2 Kings 5:16.)

38. True or false: Elisha's servant ran after Naaman and asked him for money and clothes.

39. Did Naaman give the servant any gifts?

40. True or false: Elisha was happy with the servant's actions.

10. DAVID FIGHTS GOLIATH

1. You can find the story of David's battle with Goliath in

   a) 1 Samuel

   b) The Book of David

   c) the book *Goliath: The Bigger They Are, the Harder They Fall*

   d) Jude

2. Did you know that Goliath of Gath was over nine feet tall? (See 1 Samuel 17:4.)

3. True or false: Goliath was never heavily armed. He depended on his size to protect him.

4. True or false: When Goliath challenged the Israelites to send a man to fight him, many men eagerly volunteered.

5. Why did David visit the Israelites' battlefield?

6. Before he met Goliath, David
    a) was next in line to be a high priest
    b) tended sheep
    c) was a prince of Israel
    d) learned to fight giants by jousting with a cousin

7. Gath was located in what country? Hint: Goliath was from Gath and the Israelites were battling his country.

8. True or false: While David was visiting his brothers on the battlefield, Goliath challenged the Israelites.

9. Did you know that King Saul had promised a reward to the person who killed Goliath? In addition to money, King Saul promised his daughter in marriage, and the victor's father's family would not have to pay taxes (1 Samuel 17:25).

10. True or false: David's brothers were sure David could easily slay Goliath.

11. When David heard the giant's challenge, he

    a) wondered how Goliath dared to defy the army of the living God

    b) became scared and ran home

    c) decided to videotape Goliath to show on *Real TV*

    d) threatened to take Goliath to court for saying mean things

12. Saul did not want David to fight Goliath because David

    a) already had plans to attend seminary

    b) was a consultant to King Saul on how to fix Social Security

    c) was only a boy

    d) was an old man

13. Did you know that King Saul gave David his own bronze helmet and coat of armor to use when fighting Goliath? (1 Samuel 17:38).

14. True or false: David convinced King Saul to let him fight Goliath by telling him that God had protected David from the lions and bears that attacked his sheep.

15. David took Saul's armor off, because

- a) the color bronze clashed with his dark hair
- b) Saul's armor was out of style
- c) he couldn't walk in it because he wasn't used to such cumbersome armor
- d) his friends at the mall would make fun of him for not looking cool

16. How many smooth stones did David pick up to battle Goliath?

17. True or false: When Goliath saw David coming to battle him, he shook with fear.

18. David told Goliath that his victory over him would prove that

    a) the pen is mightier than the sword

    b) he had been paying attention when he watched *Terminator 2*

    c) size means nothing

    d) there is a God in Israel

19. True or false: Goliath fell with the first stone David hurled at him.

20. After Goliath died, the Israelites

    a) chased the Philistines back to their own country

    b) offered the Philistines a permanent peace treaty

    c) slept

    d) sang "I'm in the Lord's Army!"

11. NEHEMIAH BUILDS A WALL

1. Can you find the book of Nehemiah in the Old Testament or the New Testament?

2. Who wrote the book of Nehemiah?

3. Did you know that the book of Nehemiah was written about 430 BC?

4. In Nehemiah's time, the Jews in Jerusalem were

   a) rich
   b) happy
   c) suffering
   d) in charge of Jerusalem's stock exchange

5. True or false: When the book of Nehemiah begins, the walls of Jerusalem have just been built.

6. True or false: Nehemiah asked the Lord to allow the king to have mercy on him.

7. When he heard about the people's plight, Nehemiah

    a) wept and prayed to God

    b) ran away to Tarsus

    c) recommended psychotherapy

    d) fled and ended up in the belly of a fish

8. Nehemiah was the king's

    a) food taster

    b) cupbearer

    c) jester

    d) spin doctor

9. King Artaxerxes noticed that Nehemiah

    a) had spilled wine on the palace's white carpet

    b) looked sad

    c) had the ability to interpret dreams

    d) had written him a message on the wall.

10. Nehemiah asked the king if he could

  a) give the Israelites straw to help them
     make better bricks

  b) start a program called the Great Society
     to help the Jews in exile

  c) go back and rebuild the city of
     Jerusalem

  d) grant the Jews more time off from work

11. Did the king grant Nehemiah's request?

**12. True or false: Nehemiah told the king he
was sad about Jerusalem.**

**13. Did you know that travel to Judah would
have placed Nehemiah in great danger?
Nehemiah needed letters from the king
giving him permission to pass through
enemy territory. The king also sent along
soldiers to protect Nehemiah from harm
(Nehemiah 2:7–9).**

14. The animal Nehemiah took with him was

    a) his pet goldfish

    b) his donkey

    c) a camel with bad breath

    d) a pet boa constrictor to squeeze his
       opponents to death

15. True or false: Rebuilding Jerusalem was risky because it was against the emperor's wishes.

16. Who was Nehemiah counting on for his success?

17. Did you know that King David was buried in Jerusalem? (Nehemiah 3:16).

18. The wall was built in a circle, starting and finishing at

    a) Pizza Hut of Jerusalem

    b) David's tomb

    c) a statue of Hermes

    d) the sheep gate

19. True or false: Everyone was happy to see the new wall being built.

20. True or false: When Nehemiah realized that people were making fun of his efforts to rebuild the wall, he called off the project and went back to Persia.

21. Later Jerusalem's Jews complained that

    a) they were too poor to feed their families

    b) they had gotten tired of manna

    c) there was a shortage of Kidz Bop CDs

    d) the wall should be painted gold

22. Nehemiah was angry when he discovered

    a) the leaders had been keeping all the gold paint for themselves

    b) the paint store wouldn't refund his money

    c) the rich Jews were taking advantage of their poor relatives

    d) he wouldn't be paid the thirty silver talents he had been promised

23. True or false: The leaders promised to return everyone's property and not try to collect any debts.

24. To show how God would punish any leader who didn't keep his promise to help the poor, Nehemiah

   a) shook his fist

   b) shook his sash

   c) invented a dance called the Hippy Hippy Shake

   d) told the people how to make milk shakes

25. Did the leaders keep their promise to help the poor?

26. True or false: Nehemiah took advantage of all the privileges he was entitled to as governor of Judah.

27. Why didn't Nehemiah claim his big allowance?

12. PSALM 23

1. Did you know that although Psalm 23 was written before Christ was born, it speaks of Him?

2. True or false: The book of Psalms should really be called the book of Psalm.

3. Did you know Psalms is entitled "Praises" in the Hebrew text?

4. Is the book of Psalms located in the Old Testament or the New Testament?

5. Who wrote Psalm 23?

6. True or false: David wrote all of the psalms.

7. What did David call the Lord in the first verse of Psalm 23?

8. In the Bible, Christians are sometimes referred to as

   a) goats
   b) vipers
   c) serpents
   d) sheep

9. David may have sung the psalms as he played the

   a) electric guitar
   b) tuba
   c) accordion
   d) harp

10. The Lord leads those He loves to

   a) fame in Hollywood
   b) money so they can buy anything they
      want
   c) contentment
   d) poverty

11. David writes, "Yea, though I walk through the valley of the shadow of death, I will fear no evil: for thou art with me" (Psalm 23:4 KJV). After reading this, do you think David was a young shepherd boy when he wrote this psalm, or an old man reflecting upon his life?

12. Psalm 23 contains the popular expression "my cup runneth over" (verse 5). This means the author is

   a) planning to sue a restaurant for serving too-hot coffee
   b) joyful
   c) forced to pay high dry-cleaning bills
   d) clumsy

13. In the psalm, "goodness and mercy" will follow David

   a) until he catches the flu
   b) until he gets a bad grade in school
   c) all the days of his life
   d) except on Tuesdays

13. LAMENTATIONS

1. Where in the Bible can you find the book of Lamentations?

2. Lamenting means

    a) being sorry about something

    b) being glad about something

    c) arguing

    d) singing

3. Did you know that the prophet Jeremiah probably wrote Lamentations?

4. In this book, Jeremiah laments

    a) the cancellation of God's promise to provide manna to the people

    b) the death of Moses

    c) having to eat spinach lasagna

    d) the destruction of Jerusalem in 586 BC

5. Did you know that the book of Lamentations consists of five poems?

6. True or false: The first poem is about Jerusalem's sorrow.

7. The second poem speaks of God's

   a) love
   b) anger
   c) mercy
   d) kindness

8. True or false: Although God punished Jerusalem, he brought the Jews back to Himself.

9. True or false: The fifth poem is a prayer for mercy.

10. Think about the last time you asked God for forgiveness. How did you feel? Did you know it is important to ask God for forgiveness when you do wrong?

14. JOEL

1. Did you know that the book of Joel makes no mention of any king or foreign nation? This means it is hard for Bible scholars to tell exactly when it was written. However, they believe it was written in the eighth or ninth century BC.

2. Who wrote the book of Joel?

3. You can find the book of Joel in

    a) the Old Testament, after Hosea

    b) the New Testament, before Matthew

    c) the Old Testament, after Daniel

    d) your Bible's concordance

4. Joel was a

    a) Levite

    b) prophet

    c) tax collector

    d) Hollywood director

5. True or false: A prophet tells what God plans to do in the future.

6. Joel talked about a time in the past when the land was filled with

    a) milk and honey

    b) locusts

    c) floods

    d) thieves

7. True or false: The people were upset because their crops had been destroyed by bugs.

8. The Lord wanted the people to

    a) invite Him to the Super Bowl

    b) repent of their sins

    c) stop eating fruit from the Garden of Eden

    d) build an ark

9. True or false: God restored Israel's fertile land.

10. True or false: God told the land and animals not to be afraid.

11. Why should the people be glad?

12. True or false: God will judge the nations in the Land Before Time.

13. Did you know that the term Valley of Jehoshaphat means "Yahweh judges"? The Good News Bible translates Valley of Jehoshaphat as "Valley of Judgment."

14. Egypt and Edom will be punished for attacking

    a) The United States

    b) Saudi Arabia

    c) Jordan

    d) Judah

15. Where will the Lord live when He returns to earth?

15. GOD PROMISES A NEW KING

1. Who wrote the Old Testament Book of Zechariah?

2. You can find the Book of Zechariah in the

    a) New Testament

    b) Old Testament, after Genesis

    c) Old Testament, after Haggai

    d) Old Testament, before Zephaniah, since the books are listed alphabetically

3. Zechariah was a

    a) priest

    b) prophet

    c) man of God

    d) all of the above

4. In the beginning of his book, Zechariah says

> a) the Lord has been very angry with your fathers
>
> b) your fathers were just and fair
>
> c) your fathers will be rewarded with great riches and glory
>
> d) your fathers will appear in the movie *Twelve Tribes Are Enough*

5. True or false: Zechariah was popular because he praised the Israelites.

6. Did Zechariah receive the word from the Lord that the people were to repent as the new temple was being built?

7. Another Old Testament prophet, Haggai, began his ministry in the second year of Darius's reign. (Haggai 1:1).

8. God says He will

    a) destroy Jerusalem

    b) allow Jerusalem to suffer a terrible military defeat

    c) rain manna on the people

    d) be merciful toward Jerusalem and allow the temple to be rebuilt

9. The Lord spoke to Zechariah through

    a) visions

    b) a book

    c) the Lord's Web page

    d) dreams

10. Whom does God tell Zechariah to crown king?

11. This king's name means

    a) Dude

    b) Heirless

    c) Branch

    d) Peacemaker

16. TALKING TO GOD

1. True or false: We can pray to God anytime.

2. When we pray to God, we should first
   a) praise Him
   b) ask for whatever we want
   c) ask for bad weather so school will close
   d) tell Him we haven't done anything wrong

3. What Old Testament book contains many songs and prayers?

4. Most of the Psalms were written by
   a) David
   b) Adam
   c) Moses
   d) Mary

5. Did you know when you worship and pray with other people in your congregation, it is called corporate worship? Although praying alone is important, corporate worship is one way to take part in the Christian community.

6. True or false: In Old Testament times, people never prayed directly to God.

7. True or false: Abraham's servant asked for God's guidance when he was told to choose a wife for Isaac.

8. After Isaac married Rebekah, Isaac prayed for

    a) a home gym so he could lose the weight he had gained from his wife's cooking

    b) a second wife, like so many Old Testament men

    c) permission to join the Canaanite Bowling League

    d) Rebekah to have a baby

9. Here is a portion of a prayer Moses prayed (Deuteronomy 9:26–27 NIV): "Sovereign Lord, do not destroy your people, your own inheritance that you redeemed by your great power and brought out of Egypt with a mighty hand. Remember your servants Abraham, Isaac and Jacob. Overlook the stubbornness of this people, their wickedness and their sin." What word shows that Moses worships God? Can you find the sentence of confession?

10. When we go to God in prayer, we should

    a) be humble
    b) convince Him how great we are
    c) give Him a list of our accomplishments in church
    d) tell Him all about the latest Star Wars movie

11. When we ask God for something, it is called a petition. Although God wants us to express our wants and needs to Him, our prayers should not be full of petitions without praise or thanksgiving. Not every prayer needs to have a petition. You can simply give thanks to God or praise Him.

12. **True or false: After God allowed Israel to be ruled by kings, most of the kings proved to be good.**

13. **When Jonah tried to escape God's will, he**

   a) was swallowed by a big fish
   b) proved successful in his attempt to escape
   c) told God he would go to Nineveh if He would name a Bible book after him
   d) wrote a book called *Jonah's Travels*

14. **True or false: When Jonah was in trouble, he prayed to God.**

15. **Did you know? Before Jesus was crucified, He prayed that God would change His mind about allowing Him to die in such a horrible way (Matthew 26:39). Sometimes God wants us to do something we don't want to do.**

16. **True or false: The Bible tells us Jesus had an active prayer life.**

17. Jesus often prayed

- a) loudly, so all would hear
- b) alone
- c) only with His disciples, or else others would learn how to pray
- d) only in church

18. Who were the Pharisees?

19. The Bible tells of a Pharisee who prayed

- a) loudly, boasting about his goodness
- b) silently
- c) in French, a language unheard of at that time
- d) for God to have mercy upon him

20. The tax collector

- a) applauded the Pharisee for his goodness
- b) admitted his sin and asked God for mercy
- c) said he gave even more to the treasury than the Pharisee
- d) asked the Pharisee how he could enroll in middle school

21. Why were tax collectors in Jesus' day hated and considered sinful?

22. True or false: Jesus praised the Pharisee.

23. True or false: It is all right to ask God to crush our enemies.

24. Regarding enemies, Jesus said we are to

    a) love them
    b) bless them
    c) pray for them
    d) all of the above

25. True or false: When you pray, you should always give thanks to God.

26. Name five things you can thank God for today.

17. DOVES

1. Did you know the first place a dove is mentioned in the Bible is Genesis 8:8? This is the story of the Great Flood.

2. Who built the ark to keep his family and the animals safe while God destroyed the earth with water?

3. True or false: The first bird Noah sent away from the ark was a dove.

4. Noah sent a dove out of the ark

    a) to see if the waters had gone down so they could leave the ark

    b) to find Dove Bars because they were hungry

    c) to dig up some worms for the other birds on the ark

    d) to symbolize peace in the world

5. **If Noah took in animals two by two, how could he send out a dove alone to search for receding water without wiping out the entire population of doves?**

6. **When the dove returned the first time, Noah knew**

   a) there was still too much water for them to leave the ark

   b) the Dove ice cream factory had been declared a federal disaster area

   c) there were no worms

   d) peace would not be possible just yet

7. **After the second trip, the dove brought Noah**

   a) an olive branch

   b) a bar of vanilla ice cream covered with milk chocolate

   c) a necklace

   d) a slingshot

8. **True or false: Noah waited seven days between each time he sent the dove out from the ark.**

9. **Did the dove return after the third trip?**

10. True or false: If you want to find out about the Law of Moses, you should read the Pentateuch.

11. In the Song of Solomon, the loved one is called a dove (2:14; 5:2; 6:9). What qualities do you think the loved one possesses?

12. After Jesus was baptized, the Holy Spirit descended upon Him like

    a) an angel
    b) a raven
    c) rain
    d) a dove

13. Jesus said, "Behold, I send you forth as sheep in the midst of wolves: be ye therefore wise as serpents, and harmless as doves" (Matthew 10:16 KJV). This means

    a) God will protect you from every enemy
    b) don't let anything get in your way
    c) don't dress as a sheep for a costume party
    d) be wise, but do not hurt anyone

14. **In New Testament times, Jews still made animal sacrifices to God to atone for their sins under Mosaic Law. Why don't Christians make animal sacrifices today?**

15. **True or false: Jesus approved of the process of buying and selling sacrificial doves and other animals in the temple, since it was so convenient for everyone concerned.**

16. **Moneychangers were in the temple to**

    a) provide correct change

    b) exchange one form of money for another

    c) drum up support for Euromoney

    d) take bets on races in the Coliseum

17. **Jesus said the merchants had made the temple a**

    a) Cub Scout den

    b) meeting place for den mothers

    c) den of bears

    d) den of thieves

18. NAVIGATING THE NEW TESTAMENT

1. "And Jesus said unto them, Come ye after me, and I will make you to become fishers of men" (Mark 1:17 KJV). Here Jesus was speaking to His disciples. Why is this an important verse for us today?

2. Did you know? The ancient Greek text of the Old Testament is called the Septuagint version. Most scholars believe it was recorded about two hundred years before Christ was born.

3. The number of years between the end of the Old Testament and the beginning of the New Testament is

    a) zero
    b) 400
    c) 1,000
    d) not known

4. True or false: When the New Testament was written, Israel was the largest and most powerful nation on earth.

5. **Name the first four books of the New Testament, which are also known as the four Gospels.**

6. **The four Gospels tell about**

   a) the life and ministry of Jesus

   b) Noah's ark

   c) Paul's mission work

   d) the gospel music industry

7. **True or false: Christians only need to read the four Gospels.**

8. **True or false: Jesus wrote all four Gospels.**

9. **In the four Gospels, we can find**

   a) stories Jesus told

   b) Jesus' family lineage

   c) accounts of Jesus' resurrection

   d) all of the above

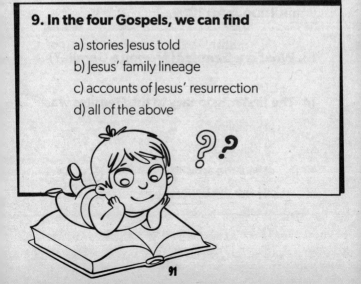

10. Who was the first person killed because he believed in Christ?

11. Some years are preceded by the abbreviation AD, which means

    a) after death
    b) Antoinette and Dominic
    c) after Domino's Pizza
    d) *anno Domini*

12. Did you know the New Testament was not put together as a collection of books until about AD 100?

13. What is a Gentile? (Are you a Gentile?)

14. The first missionary to the Gentiles was

    a) Jim Elliot
    b) Billy Graham
    c) Paul the apostle
    d) John the Baptist

15. We can read about the travels of the first missionary to the Gentiles in the book

    a) *How to Tour Asia Minor on $1 a Day*

    b) Acts

    c) *Converting the Pagans: I Did It My Way*

    d) *Finding the Hidden Elegance of Prison Food*

16. Paul the apostle wrote many letters that are included in the New Testament. They give Christians instructions on how to

    a) get revenge on the Romans

    b) send attachments by e-mail

    c) love one another, behave, and conduct church business

    d) slip a file inside a bagel so he could break out of prison

17. Why are these letters important to Christians today?

18. Throughout Paul's letters, he says Christians must have

    a) love

    b) husbands or wives

    c) riches

    d) funds to support his ministry

19. True or false: We know for a fact that Paul wrote the book of Hebrews.

20. The book of Hebrews says

    a) the Christian faith is better than all others

    b) the Jewish faith is better than the Christian faith

    c) Christians need to sacrifice two doves each Sunday

    d) no Christian should watch television on Sunday

21. True or false: The books of James; 1 and 2 Peter, 1, 2, and 3 John; and Jude are all named after the people who wrote them.

22. The epistle (or "letter") of James tells Christians how to

a) set up the Communion table

b) write a proper thank-you note

c) write a Sunday school curriculum for toddlers

d) live according to God's Word

23. How many New Testament epistles are attributed to Peter?

24. True or false: Peter is considered to be the leader of Jesus' twelve disciples.

25. 1 Peter was written to help

a) raise money for new carpet in the sanctuary

b) Christians find other Christian businesses

c) suffering Christians

d) missionaries in South America

26. True or false: According to Peter, you can trust any person who claims to be a Christian.

27. Peter wrote his second letter to help Christians

    a) decide who are false teachers

    b) determine who will be the best Bible translators

    c) decide if they want to be missionaries

    d) buy their first home

28. True or false: Both John and Jude condemn false teachers in their letters.

29. What is the last book of the New Testament?

19. THE GOSPELS

1. How many Gospels are there in the Bible?

2. In your Bible, you can find the Gospels in

  a) the first part of the New Testament
  b) the first part of the Old Testament
  c) the concordance
  d) the last part of the New Testament

3. What is a concordance?

4. The Gospels are the books of

  a) Genesis, Exodus, Leviticus, Numbers,
     and Deuteronomy
  b) Jude and Revelation
  c) Matthew, Mark, Luke, and John
  d) Genesis and Matthew

5. All four Gospels tell us about

    a) the life and ministry of Jesus

    b) Paul's life

    c) the events surrounding Joshua's prophecies

    d) how to get good grades without doing any work

6. Your Bible may have red letters in some places. What do they mean?

7. If your Bible has red letters, you can see them in the Gospels and in

    a) Genesis

    b) the Acts of the Apostles and Revelation

    c) no other book of the Bible

    d) Psalms

8. True or false: Jesus wrote parts of all four Gospels.

9. Did you know that Matthew was also called Levi? (See Mark 2:14.)

10. Matthew

a) was the disciple who betrayed Jesus

b) collected taxes for Rome

c) ran the water slide at the King's Dominion amusement park in Israel

d) was a Roman soldier

11. Matthew traces Jesus' line back to King David. Why do you think he stopped there?

12. Did you know that the book of Mark is the shortest Gospel?

13. True or false: Luke is the longest Gospel.

14. Which Gospel has the most chapters?

15. Did you know that John was one of the disciples in Jesus' inner circle? The Bible often describes Jesus taking "Peter, James, and John" away on private journeys.

20. TWO BLESSED PARENTS

1. Who were the earthly parents of Jesus Christ?

2. A listing of Jesus' ancestors, or His lineage, is found

    a) in Matthew and Luke

    b) in Mark and John

    c) in Genesis and Revelation

    d) in New York's Museum of Modern Art

3. The two sources that trace Jesus' lineage differ from David to Jesus. This is because

    a) neither one is accurate

    b) the records in Bethlehem burned

    c) one source had to guess at names after a computer crash

    d) one traces Joseph's line from David, while the other traces Mary's ancestors

4. Did you know Jesus is from the line of King David? Matthew lists Joseph as Mary's husband and Joseph was from the line of King David. Though Jesus is the son of Mary and the Holy Spirit, he is the legal son of Joseph. Therefore, Jesus is from the line of David.

5. Who told Mary she would bear a son?

6. True or false: The messenger did not know whether the baby would be a girl or a boy.

7. True or false: Mary and Joseph had been married for twenty years before she became pregnant by the Holy Spirit.

8. Joseph was a

    a) circus performer
    b) computer nerd
    c) Pharisee
    d) just, or honest, man

9. When Joseph first discovered Mary's pregnancy, he

    a) started to cry

    b) set up a website so he could post baby pictures on the Internet

    c) suggested Mary should be stoned

    d) planned to break off the engagement quietly

10. True or false: For Mary and Joseph, breaking off the engagement would not have been serious, since Mary had not purchased her wedding gown, hired caterers, or reserved the Country Club of Nazareth for the wedding reception.

11. Who convinced Joseph not to break off the engagement with Mary?

12. True or false: Joseph selected Jesus' name.

13. Why was the baby named Jesus?

14. Jesus is also called Emmanuel, meaning

    a) firstborn

    b) Christmas

    c) God with us

    d) man

15. While she was expecting Jesus, Mary visited

    a) a local herbalist

    b) her cousin Elizabeth

    c) Joseph's parents, to tell them she was sorry if they were embarrassed

    d) a free health clinic

16. True or false: Joseph immediately did what the Lord instructed.

17. Mary gave birth to Jesus in

> a) the finest medical facility available, since Jesus is the Messiah
>
> b) her home
>
> c) the car, during a traffic jam
>
> d) a stable because there was no room for them at the inn

18. Did you know Simeon, a devout man who declared Jesus the Messiah soon after he was born, told Mary she would suffer along with her son. "Then Simeon blessed them and said to Mary, his mother: 'This child is destined to cause the falling and rising of many in Israel, and to be a sign that will be spoken against, so that the thoughts of many hearts will be revealed. And a sword will pierce your own soul too' " (Luke 2:34–35 NIV).

19. True or false: Joseph and Mary reared Jesus as a Christian.

20. Did you know that when Jesus and Mary are mentioned together in the Bible, Jesus' name always appears first? (Matthew 2:11; 13–14; 20–21.)

21. Jesus performed His first miracle at

    a) Capernaum

    b) Cana

    c) Corinth

    d) Caesarea

22. The person who asked Jesus to perform this miracle was

    a) Joseph

    b) Mary

    c) Elijah

    d) a nervous bridegroom

23. This miracle was important because it strengthened the faith of

    a) Jesus' disciples

    b) Jesus' earthly mother and father

    c) His earthly sisters and brothers

    d) the townspeople of Cana

24. How many other sons did Mary have who are mentioned in the Bible? (We don't know the names of His earthly sisters.)

25. What was Joseph's profession?

26. Jesus grew up in

    a) Bethlehem

    b) Nazareth

    c) Paris

    d) Queens

27. True or false: Because Joseph and Mary were powerful and influential, Jesus was always given a hero's welcome whenever He visited His hometown.

21. THE BIRTH OF JESUS

1. True or false: The story of Jesus' birth is found in the book of Matthew.

2. Did you know there were fourteen generations from Abraham to David, fourteen from David to the exile in Babylon, and fourteen from then to Jesus' birth? (See Matthew 1:17.)

3. When she discovered she would give birth to Jesus, Mary was engaged to

   a) Adam
   b) Joseph
   c) Moses
   d) Lot

4. Did you know that Mary's fiancé was a descendant of King David? (See Luke 1:27.)

5. Who first told Mary she would have a baby?

6. True or false: Mary visited her cousin Elizabeth in Judea after she discovered she would give birth to God's son.

7. True or false: In a dream, an angel told Joseph he should not be afraid to take Mary as his wife.

8. Did you know that Jesus was born in the same town as King David? (See Luke 2:4.)

9. In which town was Jesus born

10. Joseph and Mary went to Bethlehem before Jesus was born because

    a) they were on vacation

    b) a census was being taken

    c) they won a minivan in a sweepstakes and had to go there to claim it

    d) Joseph had been offered a job as an innkeeper

11. True or false: King Herod was filled with joy when he was told the news of Jesus' birth.

12. The wise men brought Jesus gifts of

    a) gold, frankincense, and myrrh

    b) pearls, rings, and baby rattles

    c) diapers, formula, and mohair blankets

    d) earrings, spices, and a New Testament Bible

13. True or false: When Mary and Joseph arrived in town, they stayed at the best hotel.

14. The shepherds learned about Jesus' birth from

    a) a talking wolf

    b) an invitation they received to his baby shower

    c) angels

    d) Mary

**15. Did you know Luke traced Jesus'
ancestors all the way back to Adam? You
can find the record of Jesus' lineage in
Luke 3:23–38.**

**16. True or false: The wise men told King
Herod where Jesus was.**

**17. True or false: Mary selected Jesus' name
herself.**

**18. After Jesus was born, an angel told
Joseph in a dream to take his family to**

    a) Egypt
    b) Sodom
    c) China
    d) The North Pole

**19. Joseph, Mary, and Jesus stayed in Egypt
until Herod**

    a) offered Joseph a job at the palace
       paying 5,000 talents a year
    b) repented of his sins
    c) promised not to kill Jesus
    d) died

20. Did you know that Joseph was first told in a dream to go to Israel after Herod's death? In a second dream, he was told to go to Galilee. The family settled there in the town of Nazareth (Matthew 2:22–23).

21. Jesus was called a ＿＿＿＿＿＿＿ because he grew up in Nazareth.

22. Did you know that when Joseph and Mary presented the baby Jesus to the Lord, they sacrificed a pair of doves and two young pigeons? (See Luke 2:24.)

23. Mary and Joseph offered the sacrifice because
    a) it signified their love for each other
    b) they could not find a young ram to sacrifice
    c) it was required by Mosaic Law
    d) they had no silver for the treasury

24. What godly man was told he would not die before he saw the Messiah?

22. JESUS GROWS UP

1. Did you know that Luke is the only Gospel writer who tells us about Jesus' childhood? You can find the story in Luke 2:39–52.

2. True or false: The books of the Bible that tell us about Jesus' life and ministry are called the Gospels.

3. Jesus grew up in the town of

    a) Bethlehem

    b) Cairo

    c) Paris

    d) Nazareth

4. Jesus' parents went to Jerusalem every year to celebrate the

    a) birth of Jesus

    b) Last Supper

    c) Passover

    d) Super Bowl

5. After their trip to Jerusalem when Jesus was twelve, his parents discovered He was not with their group returning to their home in Nazareth. They went back to Jerusalem to look for Him. How long did it take them to find Him?

6. Joseph and Mary found Jesus

    a) in the Temple, amazing the teachers with his wisdom

    b) at the home of a relative

    c) in a small house with a sign that read LOST AND FOUND

    d) eating ice cream at a police station

7. True or false: Jesus was surprised that Mary and Joseph did not know he would be in the temple.

8. One man who was important in Jesus' earthly life was

 a) John the Baptist
 b) John the Methodist
 c) John the Presbyterian
 d) John the Lutheran

9. Did you know that when John the Baptist was born, his father planned to name him Zechariah? The Holy Spirit led his parents to name him John instead (Luke 1:59–63).

10. John the Baptist ate

 a) granola bars and yogurt
 b) tree bark and wild honey
 c) fried bees and chocolate-covered ants
 d) locusts and wild honey

11. True or false: John the Baptist preached about Jesus.

12. True or false: John the Baptist said Jesus would baptize with the Holy Spirit.

13. When John the Baptist preached about King Herod, he said that Herod

    a) was a fine king, worthy of worship

    b) had kept his promise to give every student an iPad

    c) was evil

    d) had paid John to say good things about him

14. What happened to John the Baptist after he preached about King Herod Antipas?

15. Who baptized Jesus?

16. After Jesus was baptized, the Holy Spirit came upon him in the form of

    a) a raven

    b) an angel

    c) a locust

    d) a dove

17. True or false: Jesus turned stones into bread to show the devil He was God's Son.

18. Satan tempted Jesus by asking Him to turn stones into bread because

    a) Satan's bread had burned in the flames of hell

    b) Jesus' bread would be far better than any bread Satan could make

    c) Jesus was very hungry and wanted to eat because he had not eaten for forty days

    d) Satan's bread tasted like brimstone

19. Satan told Jesus that if He was the Son of God, He ought to be able to safely jump from the top of the temple and also turn stones into bread. Do you think these were tests of Jesus' pride? Why or why not?

20. True or false: When Satan told Jesus to jump from the top of the temple, Jesus told him that we are not to test God.

21. If Jesus would worship Satan, Satan promised to give Jesus

    a) all the world's kingdoms
    b) bags of gold
    c) heaven's gates
    d) the love of a beautiful woman

22. Who helped Jesus after he was tempted by Satan?

23. Did you know that Jesus was about thirty years old when He began His ministry (Luke 3:23)?

24. Where did Jesus begin His ministry?

23. JESUS TELL US ABOUT ENEMIES

1. True or false: Jesus says we should not take revenge on our enemies, but ask God to get back at them instead.

2. Jesus says we should lend money to

    a) our enemies, without expecting anything in return

    b) our enemies, but only once

    c) only our friends, since our enemies are mean

    d) no one, since lending money is a bad practice

3. True or false: Our reward for being kind to enemies will be a slap in the face.

4. Jesus says that God

    a) shows mercy only to those who love Him

    b) remembers only those who thank Him for His goodness

    c) is kind to everyone, including the evil and unthankful

    d) will destroy our enemies if we ask Him

5. True or false: Jesus teaches that when people say mean things to you or about you, you should be kind to them anyway.

6. Jesus says this of our Heavenly Father: "For he maketh his sun to rise on the evil and on the good, and sendeth rain on the just and on the unjust" (Matthew 5:45 KJV). What does this mean?

7. A publican is a

    a) tax collector

    b) celebrity

    c) clerk at the public library

    d) teacher at the public school

8. Did you know Matthew, one of Jesus' twelve disciples, was a publican? "As he walked along, he saw Levi son of Alphaeus sitting at the tax collector's booth. 'Follow me,' Jesus told him, and Levi got up and followed him" (Mark 2:14 NIV). As you can see from the verse, Matthew was also known as Levi.

9. If we show love only to those who love us, we are no better than whom?

10. True or false: Since it was important that Jesus not damage His reputation as God's Son, He avoided associating with outcasts and sinners while here on earth.

11. Jesus teaches we should

    a) not do anything extra for our enemies but the bare minimum

    b) love our friends more than our enemies

    c) give our enemies New Testament Bibles

    d) go the extra mile for our enemies and show them much love

12. True or false: We don't have to forgive anybody who doesn't ask us for forgiveness.

13. When Jesus speaks of neighbors, He means

a) the people who live in the house next to yours
b) everyone
c) the people who live in your town
d) your enemies

14. Jesus' teaching, "Thou shalt love thy neighbour as thyself," is what He called the second commandment (Matthew 22:39 KJV). This commandment applies to everyone, including our enemies, since enemies are also neighbors, regardless of where they live. This teaching means we are not to put our interests above those of others.

15. Jesus teaches the first great commandment is

a) don't get mad, get even

b) never forget the bad things someone has done to you

c) love God with all your heart, soul, and mind

d) don't let the sun go down on your anger

16. What is the first of God's Ten Commandments?

17. Is Jesus' teaching about the first great commandment the same as the first commandment? How?

18. According to Jesus, people will know we are His disciples when we

a) get three perfect attendance pins at church

b) love one another

c) go to Vacation Bible School every year

d) listen to Christian radio stations every day

19. Which of Jesus' disciples betrayed Him? (Hint: To betray means to deliver someone to an enemy.)

20. When Jesus' disciple betrayed Him, the disciple received

    a) a free, all-expense-paid vacation

    b) a houseful of new furniture

    c) thirty pieces of silver

    d) a chance to appear on a TV game show

21. According to Matthew's Gospel, when Jesus was betrayed, He said,

    a) "Friend, wherefore art thou come?"

    b) "Verily, I am innocent!"

    c) "Why dost thou kiss me on the cheek? Gross!"

    d) "This means I'm down to eleven disciples."

24. ALL IN A DAY'S WORK

1. What is a parable?

2. Jesus taught in parables so

    a) those who didn't love God wouldn't understand His teachings

    b) He could put them together later in a book

    c) His disciples could sell the rights to them after His resurrection

    d) He would be famous

3. True or false: The disciples always understood the parables without Jesus having to explain them.

4. True or false: You can find Jesus' parables in the four Gospels.

5. Did you know the parable of the householder is recorded only in Matthew's Gospel?

6. A householder is

    a) a maid

    b) a collector of miniature houses

    c) a real estate agent

    d) the head of a house

7. This parable describes

    a) a day in the life of a stay-at-home mom

    b) the Cinderella story

    c) the kingdom of heaven

    d) the fable of the tortoise and the hare

8. What coin did the householder agree to pay each laborer for a day's work in his vineyard?

9. The coin the householder agreed to pay his workers was

    a) the value of a day's pay

    b) like a US dime

    c) the most common coin in use at that time

    d) all of the above

10. True or false: Throughout the day, the householder hired more laborers.

11. Did you know? This parable speaks of day laborers, rather than people who had permanent jobs, with the householder. Think about your life on earth in relation to living with God for eternity. We only serve God a short time here on earth, but the reward He gives us is great.

12. Late in the day, some laborers were still standing around because

    a) they were lazy

    b) they wanted to see who won the football game instead of working

    c) no one had hired them

    d) they were protesting the twelve-hour workday

13. When the householder saw that the workers were still there, he said,

    a) "Who would hire such lazy workers?"

    b) "Did the Washington Redskins or the Dallas Cowboys win the game?"

    c) "You also go and work in my vineyard."

    d) "I can't hear you!"

14. True or false: Every worker was paid for the number of hours he worked.

15. True or false: The workers were paid in order hired, from last to first.

16. When those who worked twelve hours saw that those who worked a short time received a whole day's wages, did they expect to be paid more than they were promised?

17. When the workers who had worked all day said they should receive more money, the householder told them

    a) to take their pay and go, since they were paid what they were promised

    b) he had deducted part of their pay to cover taxes and health insurance

    c) he would give each of them lunch money

    d) he was penalizing them for taking long coffee breaks

18. True or false: The householder represents God.

19. Did you know some scholars think the workers who grumbled about their pay represent the Pharisees who opposed Jesus' teachings? They might also represent Christians who are faithful all their lives but wonder why God would give an equal reward to those who found Christ late in life.

20. The order the workers were paid is important because

- a) the householder liked the latecomers best
- b) the householder wanted to get rid of the slackers
- c) it made the story harder for the Pharisees to interpret
- d) those who are last on earth are first in heaven

21. The householder's response to the grumblers is like God's in that

- a) He is powerful and can do as he wishes
- b) He is generous
- c) He is willing to accept everyone
- d) all of the above

22. The grumblers were jealous and unhappy because the householder was generous. How does the householder's generosity in paying those who worked a short time compare to God's generosity to us?

25. JESUS HEALS THE SICK

1. The Bible tells us about Jesus healing sick people in

    a) the Gospels

    b) the Old Testament

    c) Revelation

    d) the book of Restoration

2. Did you know that the first story about Jesus healing someone is in Matthew 8:1–4?

3. True or false: After He healed the sick man, Jesus commanded him to tell everyone that Jesus was the Messiah.

4. Jesus healed the Roman officer's servant by

    a) touching his cloak

    b) giving him a special medicine

    c) prescribing aspirin and fruit juice

    d) giving an order for him to be healed

5. **Did you know that Jesus praised the Roman officer for having great faith? (See Matthew 8:10–13.)**

6. **Whose mother-in-law did Jesus heal of a fever?**

7. **Jesus healed the woman's fever by**

     a) touching her forehead

     b) touching her hand

     c) giving her two aspirin and advising her to call Him in the morning

     d) telling her to bury a potato under a maple tree at midnight

8. **Did you know that after Jesus cured the woman's fever, He healed many others to fulfill a prophecy of Isaiah? (See Matthew 8:16–17.)**

9. True or false: When Jesus drove demons from people, the demons proclaimed that Jesus was God's Son.

10. True or false: Jesus healed the sick because He wanted everyone to know He was the Messiah.

11. Jesus drove a mob of demons into a

     a) herd of pigs
     b) school of fish
     c) horde of evil people
     d) rock group

12. When the local people found out that Jesus had driven the mob of demons out of a man, they

     a) feasted for a week
     b) were afraid
     c) composed a song in His honor
     d) made Jesus the town's mayor

13. True or false: After Jesus drove out the demons, the people asked Him to leave their territory.

14. What did the demon-possessed man want to do after Jesus healed him?

15. True or false: Jesus told the man to go back to his family and to tell everyone what God had done for him.

16. Did the man obey Jesus?

17. To get well from an illness she had suffered from for twelve years, a woman touched Jesus'

a) clothing
b) cup
c) feet
d) hand

18. Jesus said the woman had been cured by her

a) money
b) beauty
c) courage
d) faith

19. Did you know that when the woman was healed, Jesus was on his way to an official's house to heal a little girl?

20. True or false: When Jesus arrived at the official's house, the little girl had already died.

21. Jesus said that the child was not dead, but only _____.

22. Right after Jesus brought the little girl back to life, He healed

    a) a little boy who had only two fish and a loaf of bread for lunch

    b) two blind men

    c) three blind mice

    d) ten lepers

26. THE LORD'S PRAYER

1. Did you know you can find the Lord's Prayer in two places in the Bible? You can read it in Matthew 6:9–13 and Luke 11:2–4.

2. Can you recite The Lord's Prayer by heart?

3. Jesus taught the disciples this prayer because

   a) one of them had asked Him to teach them how to pray
   b) He was angered by their awkward prayers
   c) otherwise, they would sing psalms off-key
   d) they needed a new version for Dial-a-Prayer

4. According to the Lord's Prayer, where is God the Father?

5. What does Jesus mean when He says God's name should be hallowed?

6. What do you do to honor God's name?

7. True or false: Obeying God's commandment not to take His name in vain is one way to keep God's name hallowed.

8. True or false: In Matthew's Gospel, Jesus told them how to pray because He was angered by the hypocrites' loud praying.

9. What is a hypocrite?

10. True or False: Once you learn the Lord's Prayer, there is no need to pray on your own.

11. The Lord's Prayer says to ask God for enough food every day. Can you remember the last time you were really hungry? Does remembering this make you think about how important it is to ask God to take care of you?

12. Why is this prayer called the "Lord's Prayer"?

13. When Jesus says we should ask God to forgive us as we forgive others, He means

    a) God should forgive us whether we forgive others or not

    b) we should not owe anyone any money

    c) we should not loan anyone any money

    d) God will forgive us when we forgive others

27. THE ULTIMATE SACRIFICE

1. People who are persecuted are bothered, harassed, made fun of, annoyed, and sometimes even killed. Jesus said persecuted Christians are blessed because they will have

    a) the kingdom of heaven

    b) a supply of Rid-a-Pest

    c) revenge

    d) karate lessons

2. In what famous sermon did Jesus make this statement?

3. Jesus' statement about persecution is part of what is known as the

    a) Beatitudes

    b) Attitude Adjustments

    c) Assertive Attitudes

    d) Seattle-tudes

4. True or false: Anyone who is persecuted for any reason will be blessed.

5. According to Jesus, what group of people was persecuted in the past? (Hint: Elijah belonged to this group of people.)

6. In what book of the Bible can we read about Stephen?

7. The Book of Acts is located in the

      a) Old Testament, after Genesis

      b) New Testament, following the Gospel of John

      c) end of the New Testament

      d) end of the Old Testament

8. True or false: Stephen was an evil man.

9. What is blasphemy?

10. Did you know blasphemy was a serious charge in Stephen's time? The penalty for blasphemy was death.

11. Stephen's enemies charged him with

    a) blasphemy

    b) singing off-key in the church choir

    c) selling lottery tickets

    d) charging too much for sacrificial doves

12. True or false: The charges against Stephen were true.

13. During Stephen's trial, he looked like

    a) a guilty prisoner

    b) a bored young man

    c) an angel

    d) an angry young man

14. Stephen answered the charge against him

    a) by suing his accusers for ruining his reputation

    b) by vowing to murder his enemies

    c) by throwing himself on the mercy of the court

    d) by giving a speech in defense of Christianity

15. True or false: Stephen praised Israel during his court appearance.

16. After he spoke, Stephen saw

    a) a large Bible in the sky

    b) the Red Sea part

    c) the glory of God and Jesus at God's right hand in heaven

    d) Moses and Elijah

17. How do we know this is what Stephen saw?

18. When the court heard Stephen's speech, they were

    a) angry

    b) fearful of the Lord

    c) moved to tears

    d) so emotional, they dropped the charges

19. True or false: Stephen asked God to forgive the people who punished him.

20. Did you know Saul of Tarsus was present at Stephen's stoning? "[The members of the Sanhedrin] cast him out of the city, and stoned him: and the witnesses laid down their clothes at a young man's feet, whose name was Saul" (Acts 7:58).

21. Did Saul try to stop Stephen's stoning?

22. At the time of Stephen's death, Saul was

    a) writing letters to the Christian churches

    b) raising money for the Young Men's Mission Society at his church

    c) putting Christians in prison

    d) free on parole from prison

23. True or false: Saul of Tarsus would later become the first missionary to the Gentiles.

28. JESUS' RESURRECTION

1. True or false: You can read about Jesus' resurrection in all four Gospels.

2. Who were the three women who went to Jesus' tomb the day He arose?

3. When the women saw the tomb, they discovered that the stone covering of the opening of the tomb had been rolled back by

   a) an angel of the Lord
   b) Goliath
   c) Jesus
   d) Samson

4. The one who rolled the stone back told the women,

   a) "You will be punished for stealing the body."
   b) "Expect an earthquake."
   c) "Fear not, for Jesus has risen."
   d) "I'm tired from all that work, and I want something to eat."

5. True or false: Jesus' disciples believed the women when they told them that Jesus had risen from the dead.

6. Who went to the grave to see if what the women said was true?

7. True or false: Jesus appeared to Mary Magdalene after He arose.

8. When Jesus saw His disciples after He had risen, He said,

    a) "See, I told you so!"

    b) "Is there any bread left over from the Last Supper?"

    c) "Peace be unto you."

    d) "I really missed you these past three days."

29. LUKE TELLS US ABOUT JESUS

1. Where is Luke's Gospel located in the Bible?

2. Did you know that Luke also wrote the Acts of the Apostles?

3. Where can you find the Acts of the Apostles in the Bible?

4. True or false: Luke is the only Gospel writer to tell us anything about Jesus' boyhood.

5. Can you name all four Gospels?

6. True or false: Jesus healed many people during His ministry on earth.

7. Some important people were mad at Jesus because He ate with

     a) tax collectors and outcasts

     b) no one—He ate alone

     c) His family instead of them

     d) His favorite disciples

8. True or false: Jesus showed us it is all right to prepare food on the Sabbath.

9. To show it is all right to take care of sick people on the Sabbath, Jesus healed

     a) a man with a soccer injury

     b) schoolchildren of chicken pox

     c) a man with a paralyzed hand

     d) a computer with a virus

10. True or false: When His enemies saw Jesus healing on the Sabbath, they were happy.

11. A disciple is a

    a) follower

    b) teacher of false doctrine

    c) wife of an epistle

    d) person in charge of computer disks

12. Jesus chose twelve disciples. How many of them can you name?

13. Which famous sermon did Jesus preach soon after he chose his disciples?

14. True or false: Jesus said we should hate our enemies.

15. The King James Version of the Bible quotes Jesus as saying, "And as ye would that men should do to you, do ye also to them" (Luke 6:31). This is called the Golden Rule. What is the meaning of the Golden Rule?

16. True or false: When you see someone who is wrong, you should tell that person right away without worrying about your own faults.

17. While Jesus was visiting Simon the Pharisee, a sinful woman

    a) washed His feet with her tears

    b) tempted Him

    c) danced for Him

    d) peeled grapes and fed them to Him

18. When Simon the Pharisee saw the woman, he

    a) clapped for her

    b) invited her to eat with them

    c) asked her to marry him

    d) said that Jesus shouldn't let a sinful woman touch Him

19. True or false: Although the woman was sinful, she was trying to show Jesus how much she loved Him.

30. LUKE TELLS US WHAT JESUS SAID

1. What is a parable?

2. Jesus told many lessons in parables because

    a) He enjoyed confusing everyone just for sport

    b) He knew just how to spin a yarn

    c) everyone understood right away

    d) His disciples could understand them, but not everyone else

3. True or false: Jesus revered His mother, Mary, over everyone else.

4. When Jesus performed miracles, some people thought He was the resurrected

    a) John the Baptist

    b) Moses

    c) Paul

    d) Lot

5. What does the word *resurrected* mean?

6. True or false: Jesus predicted His own death and resurrection.

7. Did you know that once when Jesus was praying, his face glowed and his clothes became dazzling white? This is called the Transfiguration (Luke 9:29).

8. During the Transfiguration, Jesus was visited by

     a) Noah

     b) the three wise men

     c) John the Baptist

     d) Moses and Elijah

9. What did Jesus' visitors talk to Him about?

10. Did you know that after Jesus was visited during the Transfiguration, God's voice came from a cloud? God said, "This is my beloved son; hear Him" (Luke 9:35).

11. The disciples who saw the Transfiguration and heard God's voice

   a) rejoiced and told everyone right away
   b) were afraid and told no one
   c) telephoned Eyewitness News
   d) posted pictures and RealAudio on the Internet

12. True or false: Jesus' disciples wondered who would be the most important among themselves in heaven.

13. Who did Jesus say would be the most important disciple in heaven?

14. **When a person who was not a disciple cast out demons in Jesus' name, the disciples**

   a) told him to stop
   b) rejoiced
   c) told him to be wary of demons
   d) tried to take credit

15. **What did Jesus tell the disciples about the man casting out demons?**

16. **Did you know it was God's plan for Jesus' death on the cross to take place in Jerusalem? Moses and Elijah talked to him about it during the Transfiguration (Luke 9:30–31). Jesus set out for Jerusalem with God's plan in mind (Luke 9:51).**

17. **True or false: When a village in Samaria refused to receive Jesus, the disciples pleaded with Jesus to forgive the people of the village.**

18. **Concerning this village, Jesus told the disciples**

    a) to set it on fire

    b) to rename it "Petra" after Peter

    c) not to be unforgiving toward the citizens of the town

    d) He would eat the Last Supper in this town

19. **True or false: After Jesus spoke to the people in the village, they decided to let him pass through.**

20. **Did you know that Jesus chose another seventy men to go before Him into each town He would be visiting? (Luke 10:1 KJV). Some Bibles give the number as seventy-two (GNB).**

21. **When visiting the towns, Jesus told the seventy workers to take**

    a) plenty of money

    b) their credit cards

    c) an angel on each shoulder

    d) nothing

31. THE PRODIGAL SON

1. Who told the story of the prodigal son?

2. Where can you find the story of the prodigal son?

3. True or false: Like many of Jesus' stories, the parable of the prodigal son appears more than once in the Bible.

4. What does the word *prodigal* mean?

5. In the story, how many sons did the wealthy man have?

6. The younger son asked his father to

   a) give him his share of his inheritance
   b) let him marry the richest girl in town
   c) allow him to go to the skating rink with the church youth group
   d) loan him some money to go to the mall

7. An "inheritance" is

    a) a hair transplant

    b) property that is passed on when someone dies

    c) nose hair

    d) Hebrew for "cash"

8. True or false: The father did as the younger son asked.

9. The younger son

    a) invested the money in comic books

    b) bought Barry Bonds's seventy-third home run baseball

    c) wasted his money

    d) buried the money in the backyard

10. After the son's money was gone, he got a job

    a) at a fast food restaurant

    b) herding sheep

    c) as a used car salesman

    d) tending pigs

11. True or false: When the father saw the son returning, he was angry and told him to go back to tending pigs.

12. When the son returned, the father gave him

     a) a whipping

     b) a video game play station

     c) a job

     d) a ring, a robe, and sandals

13. True or false: The father threw a big party to celebrate.

14. True or false: The father was so happy to have the younger brother home, he forgot all about the older brother.

15. When the older son heard about the welcome home party, he

    a) hired a band to play at the party

    b) hugged and kissed his brother

    c) gave his brother the keys to his car

    d) was angry

16. Why did the older brother feel this way?

17. The father said to the older brother,

    a) "Leave my house."

    b) "I always liked your younger brother better than you."

    c) "Everything I have is yours and we are close."

    d) "You always were a tattletale."

18. True or false: The father tried to convinced the older brother to celebrate his brother's homecoming.

32. THE GOOD SAMARITAN

1. Where can you find the story of the good Samaritan?

2. True or false: The parable of the good Samaritan can be found in all four Gospels.

3. Did you know that the Gospel of John does not record any of Jesus' parables?

4. A parable is

    a) a biography

    b) a pair of pears

    c) a story that teaches a lesson

    d) a fable told by Aesop

5. Jesus told the story of the good Samaritan to answer the question,

  a) "Can I follow you?"

  b) "What can I eat?"

  c) "Is it okay for me to watch PG-13 movies?"

  d) "Who is my neighbor?"

6. Jesus was asked this question by

  a) a lawyer

  b) an evil woman

  c) Satan

  d) one of the seven dwarves

7. In the story, a man needed help because he

  a) had eaten too much and needed to be carried

  b) didn't know who his neighbor was

  c) had been beaten and robbed

  d) refused to ask for directions even though he had been driving for hours

8. True or false: When the priest and Levite saw the man lying on the side of the road, they stopped and helped him.

9. To what city was the man going when he was beaten and robbed? Hint: The Jews had taken it by knocking down its walls with the sound of trumpets and a shout.

10. Who stopped to help the injured man?

11. Did you know that the road to Jericho was very dangerous? Thieves and bandits could hide in its mountainous terrain, waiting to rob travelers. This is probably why it is the setting for the parable of the good Samaritan.

12. Did you know that the Samaritan was an unlikely person to help a Jew? Jews were their hated enemies. This is demonstrated by the Samaritan village that refused to offer Jesus a place to stay when they discovered He was on His way to Jerusalem. Read Luke 9:51–56 to learn more.

13. The salves the Samaritan applied to the man's wounds were

    a) Solarcaine spray and Bactine

    b) Dr. Feelgood's Miracle Salve and Potion

    c) oil and wine

    d) rubbing alcohol and butter

14. True or false: The Samaritan stayed with the man until the following day.

15. The Samaritan took the man to

    a) dinner at Burger King

    b) a dark alley and robbed him

    c) an inn

    d) a revival meeting at church

33. MARTHA

1. Did you know there is no woman by the name of Martha in the Old Testament?

2. You can read about Martha in

    a) the Gospel of John

    b) John's first epistle

    c) a book called *Martha's Vineyard*

    d) the Gospels of Luke and John

3. In what town did Martha live?

4. True or false: Martha was the sister of Lazarus, whom Jesus loved very much.

5. Martha was the sister of Mary, who

    a) had perfumed Jesus' feet and wiped them with her hair

    b) gave birth to Jesus

    c) was also known as Mary Magdalene

    d) brought her lamb to school

6. When Jesus heard that Lazarus was sick, He

> a) was convinced the sickness would end in death
>
> b) knew the sickness would be to God's glory
>
> c) diagnosed it as an upset stomach
>
> d) developed a vaccine for the sickness

7. True or false: As soon as Jesus heard Lazarus was sick, he rushed to Lazarus's house right away.

8. By the time Jesus arrived at Martha's house, Lazarus was

> a) all better
>
> b) dead
>
> c) gone to California in search of gold
>
> d) on a tour to promote his book, *Beyond Death: The Real Truth*

9. When Martha heard Jesus was visiting, she

   a) ran out to greet Him
   b) changed the bedsheets so He would have a place to sleep
   c) put on her best dress
   d) prepared vegetable and tofu lasagna

10. Meanwhile, Mary

   a) went to the market to buy some perfume
   b) washed her hair
   c) called Bethany's Pizzeria to order Jesus' favorite pizza
   d) stayed in the house

11. True or false: Martha was convinced that if Jesus had been at the house, her brother would not have died.

12. True or false: When Jesus told Martha that Lazarus would rise again, she thought He meant Lazarus would rise again at the resurrection at the last day.

13. "Jesus said unto her, I am the resurrection, and the life: he that believeth in me, though he were dead, yet shall he live: And whosoever liveth and believeth in me shall never die. Believest thou this?" (John 11:25–26 KJV). What would you have answered?

14. After Martha told Mary that Jesus had arrived, Mary

   a) spritzed on some of the perfume she had just bought
   b) quickly dried her hair with a blow dryer
   c) ran out to meet Jesus without delay
   d) stayed in the house

15. Why did those who came to comfort Mary think she had gone to cry at the grave of her brother (John 11:31)?

16. True or false: Like her sister Martha, Mary also told Jesus that Lazarus would not have died if He had been there.

17. Did you know the story of Lazarus contains the shortest verse in the King James Bible? That verse is John 11:35: "Jesus wept."

18. Why did Jesus weep?

19. The reaction in the crowd of mourners was mixed. Some marveled at how much Jesus loved Lazarus (John 11:36), while others remarked that Jesus, who had healed the blind, could have prevented Lazarus's death (John 11:37). Jesus' power was well known throughout the community.

20. The grave of Lazarus was

    a) a vault in the family mausoleum (a building holding many bodies)

    b) six feet deep

    c) in a shallow ditch

    d) a cave, with a stone rolled over the entrance

21. When Jesus asked that the grave be opened, Martha said,

    a) "Lord, by this time he stinketh: for he hath been dead four days."

    b) "Let me fetch my brothers, who art stronger than I."

    c) "Lord, it is impossible, for I have no shovel."

    d) "I cannot, for I hath lost the key to the vault."

22. True or false: Martha agreed to opening the grave after Jesus reminded her she should have faith.

23. Did Jesus raise Lazarus from the dead even though he had been dead for several days?

24. Was Martha present when her sister Mary anointed Jesus' feet with ointment and wiped them with her hair?

25. Judas Iscariot objected to Mary's costly act because the perfume could have been sold and the money

    a) given to the poor

    b) used to pay Martha for the dinner she had just catered for them

    c) given to Jesus' parents, Mary and Joseph

    d) used to buy gas for their tour bus

26. The Bible says Judas objected in truth because

a) he was taking money from the disciples' funds for himself

b) was a member of Bethany's War on Waste recycling drive

c) wanted to purchase a stretch limo for them to ride in

d) wanted the perfume for himself

27. Now that you have learned more about Judas Iscariot, are you surprised he was the disciple who betrayed Jesus?

28. Did you know that Bethany, the village where Martha lived, was only about two miles from Jerusalem?

29. True or false: Jesus visited Martha on at least one occasion.

30. When Mary did not help Martha prepare dinner for Jesus, Martha

a) did not complain

b) wouldn't speak to Mary for several days

c) asked Jesus to tell Mary to help her

d) threw a vase at Mary

31. What was Mary doing rather than helping Martha?

32. Jesus told Martha that

    a) Mary was indeed very, very lazy

    b) Mary wasn't very interesting anyway

    c) He would buy her a new vase

    d) she should allow Mary to listen to His Word

33. Jesus' response to Martha meant

    a) He liked Mary more than Martha

    b) there is a time to worry about physical needs and a time to listen to God

    c) He felt sorry for Mary

    d) she should hire a maid

34. PAUL SPEAKS ABOUT LOVE

1. Who wrote 1 Corinthians?

2. The Corinthians who received the letter were

> a) members of the Corinthian Country Club
> b) members of the church at Corinth
> c) makers of Corinthian leather
> d) reporters for the *Corinthian Courant*

3. Did you know that in some older versions of the Bible, the word *charity* is used in place of the word *love* in Paul's first letter to the Corinthians. If you have ever heard someone speak of showing another person Christian charity, it means showing kindness and compassion.

4. True or false: Fine preaching makes up for a lack of love.

5. You don't need love if you have

   a) lots of money

   b) faith

   c) plenty of lambs to sacrifice

   d) none of the above. You must have love.

6. When Paul says love is not puffed up, he means love is not

   a) fat

   b) filled with air

   c) inflated like a blowfish

   d) proud

7. What does Paul mean when he says that love is not provoked (1 Corinthians 13:5)?

8. True or false: We know everything there is to know while we live on earth.

9. Of faith, hope, and love, which is the greatest?

10. Why do *you* think love is so important?

35. THE FRUIT OF THE SPIRIT

1. The fruit of the Spirit is

   a) an orange

   b) a lemon

   c) a set of characteristics you'll have if you love God

   d) the title of a Dr. Seuss book

2. Where in the Bible can we can learn about the fruit of the Spirit?

3. Who told us about the fruit of the Spirit?

4. The Galatians were

   a) members of a group of churches in Galatia

   b) a galaxy of stars

   c) bugs from a popular video game

   d) aliens from another galaxy

5. Did you know that you cannot find Galatia on a modern-day map? Galatia was the name of a region in Asia Minor—modern-day Turkey.

6. One fruit of the Spirit is love. Can you name at least one other letter where Paul writes about love?

7. When Paul speaks of joy, he means
   a) a dishwashing detergent
   b) happiness in the Lord
   c) a baby kangaroo
   d) Joseph's nickname

8. Did you know there is more than one type of peace? You can be at peace with yourself, which means you like yourself. You can be at peace with others, which means you aren't fighting with anyone. On a national level, this means the country is not at war with another country. Most importantly, you can be at peace with the Lord. This does not mean you are perfect. When you are saved, you know the Lord has forgiven your sins. This puts you at peace with Him.

9. You are long-suffering when

   a) you can sit through math class without passing a note

   b) you don't fall asleep when the teacher is talking about history

   c) you can forgive other people when they sin against you

   d) you will eat vegetables three meals in a row

10. Paul names gentleness as a fruit of the Spirit (Galatians 5:22). Who is the gentlest person you know? What is he or she like?

11. True or false: Goodness is a fruit of the Spirit.

12. True or false: A person of faith must see something to believe it.

13. Meekness means a person is

   a) a wimp

   b) quiet

   c) strong but kind to others

   d) mousy

14. The King James Version says that temperance is a fruit of the Spirit. Temperance is

   a) another word for heating and cooling your house

   b) running a fever

   c) not going outside when it is too hot or too cold

   d) controlling yourself and not going to the extreme

15. True or false: Paul wrote about the fruit of the Spirit because he wanted everybody to live by the letter of the Mosaic Law.

16. Paul says that those living with the fruit of the Spirit have crucified the flesh. This means they

    a) have Christian tattoos

    b) have pierced their ears

    c) have skin as wrinkled as a prune

    d) don't think about their bodies as much as they think about living for Christ

17. When we walk in the Spirit, it means that

    a) we obey Christ

    b) a cloud surrounds us

    c) we play basketball in high-heeled Easy Spirit pumps

    d) Mom won't drive us to soccer practice

18. True or false: It is all right to be jealous of other people.

19. Why is it important to obey Christ?

20. Now that you have learned about the fruit of the Spirit, can you name all nine?

36. 1 PETER

1. 1 Peter is a letter written by

    a) Peter

    b) Paul

    c) Mary

    d) Moses

2. True or false: The author of 1 Peter was one of Jesus' apostles.

3. Some scholars think that Peter was the leader of the apostles because he

    a) liked to write letters

    b) is named first in every list of the apostles in the Bible

    c) had the most money

    d) was the only one with Internet access

4. Peter wrote this letter to

    a) Jesus

    b) persecuted Christians

    c) rich Christians

    d) a woman who wanted to publish his life story

5. In 1 Peter 1:4, Peter speaks of an inheritance, meaning that the people he writes to will have

    a) their fortunes told

    b) more money in the future

    c) personal hairdressers

    d) eternal life

6. True or false: Peter says that when we live like Jesus, we will not live like the rest of the world lives.

7. What does the word *redeemed* mean?

8. Peter says we were redeemed by

    a) Jesus

    b) silver

    c) a cents-off coupon

    d) the good things we do for others

9. Peter says that Christians should not envy other people (1 Peter 2:1). Which of God's Ten Commandments means the same thing?

10. We should also put aside evil speaking. What commandment does this remind you of?

11. Peter says that Christians should be like

    a) newborn babes

    b) goats

    c) sheep without a shepherd

    d) Superman

12. The milk of the word will

    a) taste sour
    b) turn to yogurt
    c) spill on your books
    d) make Christians grow

13. Peter says that Christians are like

    a) pet rocks
    b) red bricks
    c) living stones
    d) wood

14. True or false: Christians are building a spiritual house.

15. Did you know that the name Peter means "rock"?

16. True or false: Jesus is the chief cornerstone.

17. What does Peter mean when he says that Jesus is the stone of stumbling and rock of offense?

18. True or false: It is important for Christians to live as Christ wants because the world is watching us.

19. Peter calls Christians sojourners. What is a sojourner?

20. True or false: When Peter compares Christians to pilgrims, he is talking about the people who sailed to America on the *Mayflower*.

21. Christians should

    a) disobey all laws made by men
    b) obey the laws of their nations
    c) fight against the law
    d) obey the laws they think are right

22. True or false: It is all right to be mean to someone who is mean to you first.

23. When people say mean things to us, we should

a) remember how Jesus trusted God

b) gossip about them

c) take them to court and let the judge decide what to do

d) tell the teacher

24. Peter compares the Christians to

a) blocks of granite

b) diamonds

c) lost sheep

d) all of the above

25. Jesus spoke about lost sinners in three parables. Do you remember what they are?

26. Peter refers to Jesus as a shepherd. What famous psalm also says he is a shepherd?

27. What does the word *submit* mean?

28. True or false: Peter says that wives should only submit to their husbands if the husbands follow Christ.

29. Did you know that Peter offers hope to the wives of unsaved men? He tells them to obey God and to show their husbands how to live like Christians. Their lives may inspire their husbands to turn to Christ.

30. True or false: Christian women should depend completely on lipstick, perfume, and jewels to make them pretty.

31. Peter tells husbands to

    a) give their wives anything they want

    b) take their wives out to dinner three times a week

    c) give their wives a dozen roses for every wedding anniversary

    d) honor their wives

32. When Peter says that the wife is the weaker vessel, he means that the wife is

    a) not as strong physically as her husband

    b) dumb

    c) like a tiny blood vessel

    d) like a rowboat

33. True or false: A Christian husband and wife are equal in that both will be given God's gift of salvation.

34. True or false: Those who suffer because they are Christians are blessed.

35. Peter says that Christians should answer questions about the Christian faith with

    a) anger

    b) meekness

    c) a funny greeting card

    d) an e-mail message

36. Jesus spoke about suffering and meekness in a famous sermon. Do you remember the name of the sermon?

37. Did you know that when Peter says, "Love will cover a multitude of sins," this is a quote from Proverbs 10:12?

38. When Peter says that love will cover a multitude of sins, he means that

   a) sleeping sins will stay warm

   b) a sinner can take refuge in a bomb shelter

   c) love has its limits

   d) when you love people, you can forget about their sins

39. True or false: Peter says that Christians should rejoice at being tried, because they share in suffering with Christ.

40. In 1 Peter 4:15, Peter cautions Christians not to

   a) be busybodies

   b) be busy building up their bodies

   c) busy themselves listening to hard rock music

   d) watch PG rated movies

41. Who are our earthly shepherds in the church today?

42. Young people should submit to their

     a) impulse to play computer games all day

     b) elders

     c) sisters

     d) friends at school

43. The Ten Commandments say, "Honor thy father and thy mother" (Exodus 20:12). How is this commandment like Peter's advice to young people?

44. Who is the enemy of Christians?

45. What is the last word in Peter's first letter?

ANSWERS

1. The Old Testament

1. True

2. True

3. a) Pentateuch

4. Moses wrote the first five books of the Bible.

6. c) Exodus and Deuteronomy (Exodus 20:1–17; Deuteronomy 5:7–21)

7. The Ten Commandments are:
   1. Thou shalt have no other gods before me.
   2. Thou shalt not make unto thee any graven image.
   3. Thou shalt not take the name of the Lord thy God in vain.
   4. Remember the sabbath day, to keep it holy.
   5. Honour thy father and thy mother.
   6. Thou shalt not kill.
   7. Thou shalt not commit adultery.
   8. Thou shalt not steal.
   9. Thou shalt not bear false witness against thy neighbor.
   10. Thou shalt not covet.

8. a) creation of the universe (Genesis 1:1–2:7)

9. In the Old Testament, the nation of Israel was divided into twelve tribes.

10. The twelve tribes were: Judah, Issachar, Zebulun, Reuben, Simeon, Gad, Ephraim, Manasseh, Benjamin, Dan, Asher, Naphtali (Numbers 2:3–31).

11. a) God gave the laws to Moses.

12. These records are important to show family lineage. Because of these records, we can trace Jesus' family line back to Adam and Eve.

13. d) illustrates two kinds of love. Ruth's loyalty to her mother-in-law, Naomi, is an example of love of family. As a result of staying with Naomi, Ruth found romance—the second kind of love—with a godly man named Boaz.

14. b) won a beauty contest and married the king (Esther 2:2–9)

15. True. Jewish people celebrate the Feast of Purim to remember how Esther saved her people at great risk to her own life (Esther 9:26–32).

16. b) God protects and rewards those who love Him (Job 42:12–17).

17. True

18. d) sings praises to God

20. c) Proverbs

21. False

22. a) earth's glories fade, but God is forever

23. False. We don't know who wrote several books, including Job, 1 and 2 Samuel, 1 and 2 Kings, or Esther.

24. Bible scholars study a long time to understand God's Book. They use their knowledge to piece together data like a puzzle. If the name of a king, judge, or other ruler is

mentioned, we know the events took place during the time he ruled. Locations also help. For instance, since the first man and woman, Adam and Eve, were the only people ever to live in the Garden of Eden, we know their story takes place at the beginning of creation. The language of the text is also important. For example, Hebrew text was generally written earlier than Greek text. Even with all this information, we still aren't sure who wrote some of the Bible books. If you enjoy history and puzzles, perhaps the Lord will someday call you to become a Bible scholar.

25. d) one sent by God to tell His plans for the future

26. d) often is sent to warn God's people to repent of sin

2. The Cruise of a Lifetime

1. a) Genesis. The story is told in chapters 6–9.

2. False. God was angry that the people were so evil (Genesis 6:5–6).

3. b) destroy all the people, animals, and birds He had created (Genesis 6:7)

4. True (Genesis 6:9–10)

5. Noah had three sons (Genesis 6:9).

6. Noah's three sons were named Shem, Ham, and Japheth (Genesis 6:9).

8. A ritually clean beast is acceptable to God

for sacrifice. A ritually unclean beast is not. Although God asked for animal sacrifices under Old Testament law, Christians do not make animal sacrifices. Instead, we give money to the work of the church. It is also important to give our time to the church. We can do that by helping with vacation Bible school, babysitting in the nursery, or in other ways. How can you help your Sunday school teacher or other adults in church?

9. c) 600 years old (Genesis 7:6)

10. It rained forty days and forty nights (Genesis 7:12).

12. a) 7½ months. The flood began on the seventeenth day of the second month (Genesis 7:11). And Noah was able to see the tops of the mountains again on the first day of the tenth month (Genesis 8:5).

14. False. The first bird Noah sent out from the ark was a raven (Genesis 8:7).

15. d) an olive branch (Genesis 8:11). This showed Noah that the water had started to go down.

16. True (Genesis 8:13)

17. c) built an altar to God and made sacrifices upon it (Genesis 8:20).

18. True (Genesis 8:21 and 9:11)

19. God was pleased with the smell of

the sacrifices Noah made after the flood. The pleasant odor caused Him to promise not to destroy the earth by flood again (Genesis 8:20–22).

20. A rainbow reminds us of God's promise (Genesis 9:13).

3. A Towering Problem

1. The story of the Tower of Babel can be found in Genesis 11:1–9.

2. True (Genesis 11:1)

3. d) an unspecified language. Everyone spoke the same language (Genesis 11:1), but the Bible does not say what language the people spoke.

4. c) brick (Genesis 11:3)

5. True (Genesis 11:4–5)

6. d) reach to heaven (Genesis 11:6)

7. False (Genesis 11:6–7)

8. d) made the people all speak different languages so they couldn't finish the work (Genesis 11:7)

9. The story of the Tower of Babel is important because:
1. It shows us that God places limits upon mankind (Genesis 11:6).
2. It explains why we speak different languages (Genesis 11:6–9).
3. It shows how God scattered the people all over the face of the earth (Genesis 11:9).

4. God's Promise to Abraham

1. True

2. You find the story of God's promise to Abraham in Genesis 17.

3. True (Genesis 17:5)

4. Abraham was ninety-nine years old when God appeared to him (Genesis 17:1).

5. c) obey Him (Genesis 17:1)

6. b) bowed down, touching his face to the ground (Genesis 17:3)

7. A covenant is a solemn promise. For example, when we are baptized, we promise God we will follow Him.

8. True (Genesis 17:2)

9. a) a relative of a future generation

10. d) the land of Canaan (Genesis 17:8). Abraham was living in Canaan as a foreigner at that time.

11. True. The covenant applied to Abraham and to future generations as well (Genesis 17:8).

12. c) Abraham was to be the father of many nations (Genesis 17:5)

13. True (Genesis 17:6)

14. True (Genesis 17:7)

15. Abraham's wife was named Sarai before God renamed her Sarah (Genesis 17:15).

16. c) have a baby (Genesis 17:16)

17. b) laughed (Genesis 17:17). Abraham

did not think it was possible for him and his wife to be new parents because they were so old.

18. God promised a baby boy (Genesis 17:16).

19. c) was ninety years old, which is usually too old to have a baby (Genesis 17:17)

20. Abraham was ninety-nine years old when God promised him a baby (Genesis 17:17).

21. c) a person who receives an inheritance. In biblical times, the firstborn son usually was next in line for his father's position and money when the father died. This meant that after the father died, the oldest son became head of the family.

22. False (Genesis 17:19)

5. The Ten Commandments

2. False: Exodus and Deuteronomy are both Old Testament books. Exodus is the second book of the Bible and Deuteronomy is the fifth book.

3. Moses wrote the first five books of the Bible.

5. The five books of the Pentateuch are Genesis, Exodus, Leviticus, Numbers, and Deuteronomy.

6. b) Mount Sinai (Exodus 19:20)

8. b) God had brought them out of slavery in Egypt. You can read about this event in Exodus 5:1–15:21.

9. True (Exodus 20:3; Deuteronomy 5:7)

10. The First Commandment is the most important because it defines our relationship to God. God wants us to love Him, just as He loves us. If we do not love God, we cannot keep the other commandments.

11. False. The second commandment tells us not to make any idols (Exodus 20:4; Deuteronomy 5:8–9).

12. God means we are not to call His name unless we are praying to Him or worshipping Him. Think about how you would feel if people kept saying your name, attracting your attention for no reason. Would you feel angry? Would you be upset? God does not want us to call His name unless we mean to speak to Him or to praise His name.

13. d) keep holy, cease work, and remember His people's deliverance from Egypt (Exodus 20:8–11; Deuteronomy 5:12–15)

14. False (Exodus 20:8–11; Deuteronomy 5:12–15). However, Jesus said that necessary work may be done on the Sabbath (Matthew 12:1–8; Mark 2:23–27; Luke 6:1–5).

15. God wants us to rest every seventh day because He rested on the seventh day after He created the world (Exodus

20:11). By resting on the seventh day, we are honoring God by being like Him in this way.

16. We attend church on Sunday, read the Bible, rest, and otherwise follow God's instructions.

17. c) father and mother (Exodus 20:12; Deuteronomy 5:16). Our parents have an important place in our lives because God has entrusted them to care for us on earth. God wants us to give them special respect and honor. However, we should also treat our teachers, pastor, and friends with respect.

18. True (Exodus 20:13; Deuteronomy 5:17). Life belongs to God the Creator, not to us.

19. We can find out how God established marriage in Genesis 2:21–34.

20. c) steal (Exodus 20:15; Deuteronomy 5:19). Showing love for others includes respecting the things they own. That is why we should not rob people.

21. We should not lie, but tell the truth. Giving false information is a sin against the person we're lying to. Lies hurt other people. A liar is not showing love to God or to other people.

23. d) wish we had our neighbor's stuff. Do you know someone who would like something you have, such as an iPad or a bike? Why not share it with that person? You may make a new friend.

24. a) Leviticus

25. b) stone tablets
(Deuteronomy 5:22)

26. False. While Moses
was with God on
the mountain for
forty days, the
people made a
false idol. Moses
was so angry with
their disobedience
to God, he broke
the tablets when
he came down
the mountain
(Deuteronomy 9:17).

27. These are the Ten
Commandments:
1. Worship no god
but God.
2. Do not worship
idols.
3. Do not take the
Lord's name in vain.
4. Remember the
Sabbath day and
keep it holy.
5. Honor your
mother and father.
6. Do not murder.

7. Do not commit
adultery.
8. Do not steal.
9. Do not lie.
10. Do not covet.

6. Joshua's Famous Battle

2. True (Numbers 27:18–23)

3. c) the death of Moses

4. The book of Joshua
is found in the Old
Testament.

5. As its title suggests,
Joshua wrote the
book of Joshua.

6. c) Jordan River (Joshua
1:2)

7. True (Joshua 1:9)

8. c) the home of a
wicked woman
(Joshua 2:1)

9. True (Joshua 2:2–7)

11. a) on the roof (Joshua 2:6)

13. True (Joshua 2:10–14)

14. Rahab protected the spies because she knew they were there to claim the land for the Lord's people (Joshua 2:9).

16. The ark of the covenant was a wooden box covered with gold and built to God's specification. It contained the stone tablets on which the Ten Commandments were written.

17. A total of 40,000 men crossed the plains of Jericho, ready to fight for the Lord (Joshua 4:13).

18. b) eaten food grown in the promised land (Joshua 5:11)

19. Manna was the food God rained down upon the Israelites to provide food for them while they were wandering in the wilderness on their way to the promised land. God rained fresh manna for them every day (Exodus 16:14–18).

20. False. The walls came tumbling down by the sounds of horns and a shout. The priests blew horns for seven days as they walked around the city with the ark of the covenant (Joshua 6:3–16).

21. The lives of Rahab and her household were spared during the fall of Jericho. This is important because it shows God always keeps his promises (Joshua 6:17, 22–23).

22. b) put into the Lord's treasury (Joshua 6:19)

23. True (Joshua 6:27)

7. Not Exactly Judge Judy

1. In the book of Judges.

3. False. Deborah was an exception.

4. d) prophet (Judges 4:4)

5. False (Judges 4:1)

6. a) made life very hard for the Israelites (Judges 4:3)

7. King Jabin had 900 iron chariots (Judges 4:3).

8. They were slaves to King Jabin for twenty years (Judges 4:3).

9. They were doing "evil in the eyes of the LORD" (Judges 4:1 NIV). Though God punishes those who do evil, He also forgives those who ask for forgiveness and repent of their sins.

10. True (Judges 4:6)

11. c) deliver the enemy into the hands of Israel's general (Judges 4:6–7)

12. Mount Tabor was located in Galilee, on the borders of Naphtali and Zebulun. Some of the men in the army who were to defeat Sisera were from Naphtali and Zebulun.

13. c) a general in Israel's army (Judges 4:6–7)

14. a) Deborah, to ensure success.

Deborah had already proposed taking 10,000 men, but Barak was afraid of defeat, even with such a large army (Judges 4:8).

15. b) a woman (Judges 4:9)

16. False. Men were the heads of Jewish households. Women could not speak for themselves in legal matters. Women were spoken for by their fathers, husbands, sons, or closest male relative.

17. Yes (Judges 4:16)

18. a) the fifth chapter of Judges

8. Meet Elijah

1. a) 1 Kings (17:1)

2. c) a prophet

3. True (1 Kings 17:1)

4. d) no rain for the next few years until God commanded rain to fall (1 Kings 17:1)

5. God was angry with King Ahab because he was evil (1 Kings 16:30).

6. False (1 Kings 16:30)

7. b) worshipped the god Baal (1 Kings 16:31–32)

9. c) east of Jordan (1 Kings 17:3)

10. a) Elijah's prophecy had made King Ahab mad.

11. a) ravens (1 Kings 17:4)

12. God controls the earth and every creature living here. He has the power to command any being to do His bidding.

13. d) bread and meat in the morning and evening (1 Kings 17:6). The Bible does not tell us what kind of bread and meat the ravens brought.

14. b) a widow (1 Kings 17:9)

15. The brook dried up because, as God had promised, there was no rain (1 Kings 17:7).

16. False (1 Kings 17:12–14)

17. d) prayed to God (1 Kings 17:21). This is the same widow who had fed Elijah while he was in hiding.

18. True (1 Kings 17:23)

19. d) all of the above (Matthew 16:14). This answer (see also Mark 8:28; Luke 9:19) given by Jesus' disciples shows there was confusion about Jesus. Since He healed people and performed miracles, some thought Jesus was one of the prophets risen from the dead. The confusion is especially evident when you remember that Jesus was born six months *after* John the Baptist (Luke 1:41) and was baptized by him (Matthew 3:13; Mark 1:9). Since they lived on earth at the same time, there is no way Jesus could have been John the Baptist. The disciples knew who Jesus was, however. We are to remember Peter's answer: "And Simon Peter answered and said, Thou art the Christ, the Son

of the living God"
(Matthew 16:16 KJV).

20. True (Matthew
    17:1–3). This miracle
    of God is called the
    Transfiguration.

21. The disciples answer
    this with a question
    they asked Jesus:
    "The disciples asked
    him, 'Why then do
    the teachers of the
    law say that Elijah
    must come first?' "
    (Matthew 17:10
    NIV). The return of
    Elijah, a revered Old
    Testament prophet,
    was to signal the
    coming of the Jewish
    Messiah.

22. True. These are Jesus'
    own words: "But I
    say unto you, That
    Elias is come already,
    and they knew him
    not, but have done
    unto him whatsoever
    they listed" (Matthew
    17:12 KJV). This means

John the Baptist
was the Elijah, but
the people did not
recognize him.

9. Elisha Performs
Many Miracles

1. False (1 Kings 19:19)

2. b) 2 Kings

4. Enoch was taken to
   heaven without
   dying because he
   walked with the Lord
   (Genesis 5:23–24).

5. True (2 Kings 2:9)

6. b) dividing the Jordan
   River and walking
   on dry land (2 Kings
   2:14). He struck the
   water with Elijah's
   cloak, and the water
   parted.

7. True (2 Kings 2:15). This
   is important because
   their recognition
   of him helped to

establish Elisha as a prophet.

8. c) made the water pure (2 Kings 2:20–22)

9. c) bald (2 Kings 2:23)

10. c) rebelled against Israel (2 Kings 3:5)

11. True (2 Kings 3:16)

12. c) they thought the water they saw around the camp was blood (2 Kings 3:21–23). When the Moabites saw water on what had been dry land, they thought it was blood because the sunlight hit it in such a way that the water appeared to be red. They thought the three armies had killed each other, so they decided to rob the camp.

13. They were attacked by the Israelites (2 Kings 3:24).

14. True (2 Kings 3:24–25)

15. a) was in debt (2 Kings 4:1)

16. d) a small jar of olive oil (2 Kings 4:2). Elisha told her to get jars from her neighbors and pour the oil into them (2 Kings 4:3).

17. The woman poured the small amount of olive oil she had in her house into all the jars. When they were all filled, the oil stopped.

18. True (2 Kings 4:7). She sold the oil for money.

19. No, she did not accept his offer (2 Kings 4:13).

20. b) promising her that she would have a baby (2 Kings 4:17). The woman was rich, but she had no son. She gave birth to a baby boy as Elisha had promised.

21. c) setting up a room for him to stay in when he visited (2 Kings 4:10).

22. True (2 Kings 4:18–37)

23. a) brought the boy back from the dead (2 Kings 4:18–37)

25. This miracle might make you think of Jesus feeding 5,000 men, plus untold women and children, with the contents of a small boy's lunch. Read about it in Matthew 14:13–21; Mark 6:30–44; Luke 9:10–17; and John 6:1–14.

26. True (2 Kings 4:38-41). There had been a famine, so food was scarce. The cook used poisonous gourds by mistake. Elisha made the stew pure so they could eat it.

27. False (2 Kings 5:1). Naaman was a respected *Syrian* commander.

28. a) leprosy (2 Kings 5:1)

29. A servant girl suggested that Elisha could cure Naaman (2 Kings 5:2–3).

30. c) "I do not have the power of God! The Syrian king wants to quarrel with me" (2 Kings 5:7).

31. True (2 Kings 5:8)

32. a) wash seven times in the Jordan River (2 Kings 5:10)

33. b) was angry (2 Kings 5:11). He did not understand why he could not wash himself in a river in Damascus and become cured there.

34. False. Naaman was cured as soon as he rose from bathing in the Jordan River the seventh time (2 Kings 5:14).

35. Naaman vowed to worship Elisha's God (2 Kings 5:18).

36. d) two mule loads (2 Kings 5:17)

38. True (2 Kings 5:22)

39. Yes. Naaman gave Gehazi 6,000 pieces of silver rather than the 3,000 he asked for, plus the two changes of clothes that Gehazi requested (2 Kings 5:23).

40. False (2 Kings 5:26). Elisha rebuked him for his greed.

10. David Fights Goliath

1. a) 1 Samuel. Look in chapter 17, verses 1–54.

3. False (1 Samuel 17:5–7). Goliath wore bronze armor all over his body. A soldier went before him to carry his shield. Goliath carried a large spear.

4. False (1 Samuel 17:11). They were too scared to fight Goliath.

5. David was taking food to his three older brothers who were soldiers in battle (1 Samuel 17:17).

6. b) tended sheep (1 Samuel 17:15)

7. Gath was located in Philistia.

8. True (1 Samuel 17:23)

10. False. Eliab, the oldest, scolded David and asked him who was tending his sheep (1 Samuel 17:28).

11. a) wondered how Goliath dared to defy the army of the living God (1 Samuel 17:26)

12. c) was only a boy (1 Samuel 17:33)

14. True (1 Samuel 17:36)

15. c) he couldn't walk in it because he wasn't used to such cumbersome armor (1 Samuel 17:39)

16. David picked up five stones (1 Samuel 17:40).

17. False. Goliath made fun of David (1 Samuel 17:43–44).

18. d) there is a God in Israel (1 Samuel 17:46)

19. True. The stone hit his forehead and Goliath fell face down to the ground (1 Samuel 17:49).

20. a) chased the Philistines back to their own country (1 Samuel 17:52).

11. Nehemiah Builds a Wall

1. The book of Nehemiah is found in the Old Testament.

2. As the title suggests, the book was written by Nehemiah.

4. c) suffering (Nehemiah 1:3)

5. False. The walls had been destroyed, which is why Nehemiah was called upon to undertake building the wall.

6. True (Nehemiah 1:11)

7. a) wept and prayed to God (Nehemiah 1:4–11)

8. b) cupbearer (Nehemiah 1:11). This was an important position that put Nehemiah in the king's presence every day.

9. b) looked sad (Nehemiah 2:3). Nehemiah had never before looked sad, so the king asked him if he was sick. Nehemiah told the king his people were unhappy.

10. c) go back and rebuild the city of Jerusalem (Nehemiah 2:5)

11. Yes, the king granted Nehemiah's request (Nehemiah 2:7).

12. True (Nehemiah 2:3)

14. b) his donkey (Nehemiah 2:12)

15. True (Nehemiah 2:19)

16. Nehemiah counted on God (Nehemiah 2:20).

18. d) the sheep gate (Nehemiah 3:1, 32)

19. False. In fact, people tried to stop the work many times. Enemies made fun of the wall builders (Nehemiah 2:19; 4:1–3); they threatened an attack (Nehemiah 4:7–23); enemies tried to distract Nehemiah

from the project
(Nehemiah 6:1–4);
people tried to
ruin Nehemiah's
reputation
(Nehemiah 6:5–9,
10–14); finally,
letters were sent to
Nehemiah to scare
him into stopping the
project (Nehemiah
6:17–19).

20. False. He prayed
to God, and the
enemies' plans
to sabotage the
project were halted
(Nehemiah 4:14–15).

21. a) they were too poor
to feed their families
(Nehemiah 5:2)

22. c) the rich Jews were
taking advantage of
their poor relatives
(Nehemiah 5:7).
They were forcing
them to pay high
taxes. They also
loaned them money
to be paid back with

interest, a practice
that was against
the Jewish religion.
Some people were
so poor that they had
to sell themselves
into slavery
(Nehemiah 5:4–6).

23. True (Nehemiah 5:12)

24. b) shook his sash
(Nehemiah 5:13)

25. Yes (Nehemiah 5:13)

26. False (Nehemiah
5:15–16). Nehemiah
did not tax his
people or buy
property for himself.

27. Nehemiah knew that
the people already
had enough burdens
without him claiming
a large amount of
money and land for
himself (Nehemiah
5:18). This is in
contrast to the way
the rich Jews were
treating their relatives
in Jerusalem.

12. Psalm 23

2. False. The book of Psalms should be referred to in the plural (meaning more than one) since it contains many individual psalms (such as Psalm 23).

4. In the Old Testament, after Job.

5. King David

6. False. Although he wrote more than seventy of the psalms, others contributed to this book. Some of the authors are anonymous.

7. a shepherd (Psalm 23:1)

8. d) sheep (Matthew 25:31–34)

9. d) harp (1 Samuel 16:23)

10. c) contentment (Psalm 23:2). As a shepherd leads his sheep to a safe resting place, food (lie down in green pastures), and drink (still waters), so Jesus meets the needs of Christians.

11. Although Bible scholars have not been able to pinpoint the exact date of authorship, we can assume that the psalm was written late in David's life since he seems to think his death will happen soon. The psalm is filled with the kind of wisdom gained from living a full and long life.

12. b) joyful. His happiness and prosperity is so great, he has more than he could possibly need.

13. c) all the days of his life (Psalm 23:6). Like David, we all make mistakes. But if we believe in Jesus, God has promised never to leave us. He will truly love us all the days of our lives.

13. Lamentations

1. The book of Lamentations is found in the Old Testament after the book of Jeremiah.

2. a) being sorry about something

4. d) the destruction of Jerusalem in 586 BC

6. True (Lamentations 1)

7. b) anger (Lamentations 2)
8. True (Lamentations 3:57–58)

9. True (Lamentations 5)

14. Joel

2. Joel wrote the book of Joel.

3. a) the Old Testament, after Hosea

4. b) prophet
5. True

6. b) locusts (Joel 1:4)

7. True (Joel 1:4). A plague of locusts had invaded the land.

8. b) repent of their sins (Joel 2:12)

9. True (Joel 2:18–19)

10. True (Joel 2:21–23)

11. The people should be glad because of what God had done for them. They will have plenty to eat and will never be hated again (Joel 2:25–27).

12. False. God will judge the nations in the Valley of Jehoshaphat (Joel 3:2).

14. d) Judah (Joel 3:19)

15. The Lord will live on Mount Zion (Joel 3:21).

15. God Promises a New King

1. Zechariah.

2. c) Old Testament, after Haggai

3. d) all of the above

4. a) the Lord has been very angry with your fathers (Zechariah 1:2)

5. False (Zechariah 1:1–6). He called them to repent from the wicked ways of previous generations.

6. Yes (Ezra 6:1–15). We know this because he speaks late in the second year King Darius ruled, and King Darius allowed the temple building to resume.

8. d) be merciful toward Jerusalem and allow the temple to be rebuilt (Zechariah 1:16)

9. a) visions. Note: Dreams occur while the person is asleep, and visions occur when the person is awake. The Lord used symbols to show Zechariah, when he was fully awake, His plan for His people. Zechariah asked the angel who visited him what the symbols meant. The book of Zechariah is easier to understand

than some other books relying on symbols, such as Revelation. Read the first six chapters of Zechariah to find out all the details of the visions. Talk to another Christian about this book and its symbols.

10. Joshua (Zechariah 6:11). Note: This is not the same Joshua of the book of Joshua.

11. c) branch (Zechariah 6:12)

12. c) branch out from his place and rebuild the temple (Zechariah 6:12)

16. Talking to God

1. True. God listens to us any time of the day or night. Sometimes we might say a quick prayer when we need help. Other times we might utter a short prayer of thanks for a beautiful day or a special blessing. Still on other occasions God may lead us to say a prayer even though we weren't thinking of praying to Him even moments before. No matter how many quick prayers we say during the day, though, it is always good to take time with the Lord each day for a time of unhurried prayer.

2. a) praise Him. God likes for us to glorify and praise Him. This is shown by the many sacrifices He required in the Old Testament.

3. The book of Psalms.

4. a) David

6. False. Check out
   Genesis 24:12;
   25:21; and 1 Samuel
   8:6. And there
   are many more
   examples!

7. True (Genesis 24:12)

8. d) Rebekah to have a
   baby (Genesis 25:21)

9. The word "sovereign"
   shows Moses knows
   God is ruler over
   all. "Overlook the
   stubbornness of
   this people, their
   wickedness and their
   sin" shows he knows
   the people of Israel
   had been sinful.

10. a) be humble. Each
    and every one of us is
    lowly in comparison
    to God. By admitting
    this to God, we are
    showing Him we
    know He is great.

12. False. Most of them
    proved to be wicked.
    You can read about
    the kings of Israel in
    1 and 2 Kings and in
    1 Chronicles.

13. a) was swallowed by a
    big fish (Jonah 1:17)

14. True (Jonah 2:1)

16. True (see Mark 1:35 as
    one example). Jesus
    got up before the
    sun rose to spend
    time alone with God.
    This may have been
    the only time He had
    to be alone with God
    the Father during an
    average day.

17. b) alone (Luke 5:16)

18. Pharisees were
    members of a Jewish
    group who loved the
    Law of Moses. They
    tried to adhere to
    it and enforce it "to
    the letter." Because

Jesus overruled some of the points of this law, He angered the Pharisees.

19. a) loudly, boasting about his goodness (Luke 18:11)

20. b) admitted his sin and asked God for mercy (Luke 18:13)

21. In Jesus' day, tax collectors often charged people more money in taxes than they owed. The tax collectors then pocketed the difference. People resented the tax collectors for becoming rich through such dishonesty.

22. False (Luke 18:14)

23. False (Matthew 5:38–39)

24. d) all of the above (Matthew 5:43–44)

25. True. When you pray to God, always remember to thank Him for His goodness and mercy as well. There are many examples of thanks given in prayer in the Bible. They are most evident in Psalms since that is a book of praise and prayer.

17. Doves

2. Noah built the ark, according to God's instructions (Genesis 7:5)

3. False (Genesis 8:7). The first bird Noah sent was a raven.

4. a) to see if the waters had gone down so they could leave the ark (Genesis 8:8)

5. God provided seven pairs of some species (Genesis 7:2–3). Also, since the ark was adrift for almost a year, it is possible that babies were born on the ark.

6. a) there was still too much water for them to leave the ark (Genesis 8:9)

7. a) an olive branch (Genesis 8:11)

8. True (Genesis 8:10, 12)

9. No (Genesis 8:12)

10. True. These are the first five books of the Old Testament. Most of Mosaic Law is recorded in Exodus and Leviticus.

11. The loved one most likely is calm, gentle, tender, and peaceful.

12. d) a dove (Matthew 3:16)

13. d) be wise, but do not hurt anyone

14. Through His crucifixion, Jesus served as the perfect Lamb, the ultimate sacrifice, and washed away our sins. As a result, Christians do not need to make animal sacrifices to God.

15. False (Mark 11:15)

16. b) exchange one form of money for another. According to Bible scholars, this allowed foreigners to exchange their form of money for the kind needed to pay the temple tax.

17. d) den of thieves (Mark 11:17)

18. Navigating the New Testament

1. If we spread the Gospel and tell others about Christ, we, too, will become fishers of men.

3. b) 400. This is called the "intertestamental" period, or the silent years. During this time, society changed so that the New Testament world was much different from the Old Testament world. This explains why the New Testament was written in different languages and reflects different customs.

4. False. Israel was no longer an independent nation but a province of a larger empire.

5. The four Gospels are Matthew, Mark, Luke, and John.

6. a) the life and ministry of Jesus

7. False (2 Timothy 3:16). God speaks to us through all the books of the Bible. We must know His entire Word to be faithful.

8. False. Jesus did not write any of the Gospels.

9. d) all of the above

10. Stephen (Acts 7:59)

11. d) *anno Domini. Anno Domini* means "in the year of the Lord." This means the year falls in the Christian era, after the birth of Christ.

13. A Gentile is a non-Jew. In Jesus' time, since most Gentiles

worshipped false
gods, the Jewish
people looked
down upon them as
pagans.

14. c) Saul, later known as
Paul the apostle (Acts
9:10–15)

15. b) Acts (or "the Acts of
the Apostles")

16. c) love one another,
behave, and conduct
church business

17. Even though they
were written almost
two thousand years
ago, the instructions
contained in Paul's
letters are still timely.
For example, we
should always love
one another. How
we present ourselves
as individuals and as
members of a church
is a witness for Christ.
The world watches
us. We must live as

Christ wants us to
live—and Paul tells us
how.

18. a) love (1 Corinthians
13:1–13)

19. False. Bible scholars
are not sure who
wrote the book of
Hebrews.

20. a) the Christian faith is
better than all others

21. True

22. d) live according to
God's Word

23. Two New Testament
epistles: 1 and 2
Peter

24. True (Matthew 16:18)

25. c) suffering Christians

26. False (2 Peter 2:1)

27. a) decide who are
false teachers

28. True

29. Revelation

19. The Gospels

1. The Bible has four
   Gospels: Matthew,
   Mark, Luke, and
   John.

2. a) first part of the New
   Testament

3. A concordance is a
   list of words you
   can find in certain
   Bible verses. For
   instance, if you want
   to find out where
   the Bible talks about
   love, you can look
   up the word *love*
   in a concordance.
   The concordance
   should have a list of
   verses with the word
   love in them. Look
   in the back of your
   Bible. Does it have
   a concordance?

You can use it the
next time you want
to find a verse. The
concordance in the
back of your Bible
will not be complete
because a complete
concordance would
make your Bible
too big to carry to
church. A big book
called an "exhaustive
concordance" will
list every verse and
word, and might be
a good study tool to
help you learn even
more about your
Bible.

4. c) Matthew, Mark,
   Luke, and John

5. a) the life and ministry
   of Jesus

6. The red letters mean
   that those words
   were spoken by Jesus
   Himself. Many King
   James Version Bibles
   print Jesus' words

in red. Some new
versions do not.

7. b) the Acts of the
Apostles and
Revelation (see Acts
1:4–5, 7–8, 9:4–6,
10–12, 15–16; 11:16;
18:9–10; 20:35;
22:7–8, 10, 18, 21;
23:11; 26:14–18,
and Revelation 1:8,
11; 1:17–3:22; 22:7,
12–13, 16, 20)

8. False. Although Jesus
is quoted in all four
Gospels, He did not
actually write any
part of them.

10. b) collected taxes for
Rome

11. Matthew traced Jesus'
lineage back to King
David because he
wanted to show us
that Jesus is King.
Jesus is worthy of our
worship.

13. True

14. Although it is not the
longest Gospel, the
book of Matthew is
the Gospel with the
greatest number of
chapters (28).

20. Two Blessed Parents

1. Mary and Joseph

2. a) in Matthew and Luke
(Matthew 1:1–16;
Luke 3:23–38)

3. d) one traces Joseph's
line from David,
while the other traces
Mary's ancestors.
Matthew traces
Joseph's line, while
Luke traces Mary's. In
a time when lineage
was traced only
through men, going
back through Mary's
line was unusual.
Some scholars think

this is because Luke wanted to emphasize Mary's importance. Joseph's line shows Jesus' legal lineage since Jesus was legally recognized as Joseph's son. His blood lineage is traced through Mary. If you answered that neither source is accurate, remember that the Bible is the true, inspired, inerrant word of God!

5. an angel (Luke 1:28)

6. False (Luke 1:32)

7. False. Mary and Joseph were engaged to be married.

8. d) just, or honest, man (Matthew 1:19)

9. d) planned to break off the engagement quietly (Matthew 1:19). Note: It is important to understand that Mary had not violated any marriage or engagement vows. God chose a righteous woman to bear His son, not someone who would disregard His commandments.

10. False. An engagement was more difficult to break than it is today. As Matthew 1:19 indicates, Mary would have been disgraced if the engagement were broken.

11. Either "an angel" or "God" would be correct, since angels are God's messengers (Matthew 1:20).

12. False (Matthew 1:21). The angel told

Joseph what Jesus' name would be.

13. The name Jesus means "Savior," or one who shall save His people from their sins (Matthew 1:21).

14. c) God with us (Matthew 1:23)

15. b) her cousin Elizabeth (Luke 1:39–40)

16. True (Matthew 1:24)

17. d) a stable because there was no room for them at the inn (Luke 2:7)

19. False. Jesus was reared in the Jewish faith. Christianity was not established until after Jesus' resurrection.

21. b) Cana (John 2:1)

22. b) Mary (John 2:3)

23. a) Jesus' disciples (John 2:11)

24. four (Matthew 13:55)

25. He was a carpenter (Matthew 13:55; Mark 6:3).

26. b) Nazareth

27. False (Matthew 13:55–58)

21. The Birth of Jesus

1. True. The story of Jesus' birth is also found in Luke.

3. b) Joseph (Matthew 1:18)

5. An angel of the Lord first told Mary she would have a baby (Luke 1:28–33).

6. True (Luke 1:39–40)

7. True (Matthew 1:20)

9. Jesus was born in Bethlehem (Luke 2:5–7).

10. b) a census was being taken (Luke 2:1–3). A census is a count of how many people are living in a place at a certain time in history. The United States government takes a census of everyone in the country every ten years. Looking at old census records is one way to find out about your own ancestors.

11. False (Matthew 2:1–3). King Herod was jealous of the new baby because Jesus was called King of the Jews.

12. a) gold, frankincense, and myrrh (Matthew 2:11)

13. False. There was no room for them in the inn (Luke 2:7).

14. c) angels (Luke 2:8–14)

15. False (Matthew 2:12). God warned them in a dream not to go back to King Herod. They returned to their country by another road.

16. False. She had been told what to name Jesus (Luke 2:21).

17. a) Egypt (Matthew 2:13)

18. d) died (Matthew 2:14–15)

19. Nazarene (Matthew 2:23). This is in keeping with the word of the prophets about the Messiah.

20. c) it was required by Mosaic Law (Luke 2:24). The

freedom we enjoy as Christians did not come about until after Jesus' ministry and resurrection.

24. Simeon (Luke 2:25). Upon seeing the baby, Simeon told Mary and Joseph that Jesus was the Messiah.

22. Jesus Grows Up

2. True

3. d) Nazareth (Luke 2:39)

4. c) Passover (Luke 2:45)

5. It took Mary and Joseph three days to find Jesus (Luke 2:45).

6. a) in the Temple, amazing the teachers with his wisdom (Luke 2:46)

7. True (Luke 2:49). He answered them, "How is it that you sought me? Wist ye not that I must be about my Father's business?" (KJV). This means, "Why did you look for me? Didn't you know I was doing my Father's work?"

8. a) John the Baptist. Before John the Baptist was born, he jumped for joy upon hearing of Jesus' impending birth (Luke 1:41). He baptized Jesus (Matthew 3:13–17; Mark 1:9–11; Luke 3:21–22; John 1:31–34). Jesus spoke about John the Baptist after John's death (Matthew 11:12–19; Luke 7:19–35).

10. d) locusts and wild honey (Mark 1:6)

11. True (Matthew 3:11-12)

12. True (Mark 1:8)

13. c) was evil (Luke 3:19)

14. He was put into prison (Luke 3:20).

15. John the Baptist (Matthew 3:13–17; Mark 1:9–11; Luke 3:21–22; John 1:31–34)

16. d) a dove (Luke 3:21–22)

17. False. Instead, Jesus told Satan that people need more than bread. They also need God's word (Matthew 4:4).

18. c) Jesus was very hungry and wanted to eat because he had not eaten for forty days (Matthew 4:1–3). Satan thought Jesus' hunger would cause Him to give in to this temptation. Satan was mistaken.

19. If you think that Satan challenged Jesus in these ways to see whether Jesus was prideful, you are probably right. Pride is responsible for many sins. Satan often uses human pride in his tests. By telling Jesus He could prove He was God's Son by performing miracles, Satan hoped Jesus' pride would cause Him to fail the tests. By resisting Satan, Jesus showed us that God is more important than our own pride.

20. True (Matthew 4:5–7)

21. a) all the world's kingdoms (Matthew 4:9)

22. Angels helped Jesus after He was tempted by Satan (Matthew 4:11).

24. Jesus began His ministry in Galilee (Luke 4:14).

23. Jesus Tells Us about Enemies

1. False (Luke 6:35)

2. a) our enemies, without expecting anything in return (Luke 6:35)

3. False (Luke 6:35). Sometimes when you are nice to your enemies, you may feel as though your reward is even more insult and injury. Since this is a fallen world, people are not always nice to you just because you are nice to them. However, sometimes God allows you to receive an earthly reward when a person you are nice to changes his or her mind and becomes your friend. Whether or not this happens, though, those who follow Jesus' teachings will be rewarded in heaven as He promises.

4. c) is kind to everyone, including the evil and unthankful (Luke 6:35)

5. True (Matthew 5:45). Since this teaching goes against the ways of the sinful world, it is probably best to bless your enemies in private. Pray alone to God about them. Talk about it with another Christian you trust.

6. This means that God does not favor one person over another.

7. a) tax collector

9. Jesus says we are
   no better than
   the publicans,
   some of the most
   hated people of
   His time (Matthew
   5:46–47). Publicans
   were known for
   charging too much
   tax and keeping
   the extra money
   for themselves. In
   addition, publicans
   worked for the
   Roman government,
   which was ruled by
   people who did not
   love the Lord. Just
   like it was easy for the
   publicans to rob the
   people, so it's easy
   for us to love only
   those who love us.
   Jesus wants us to take
   the extra step and be
   kind to people who
   don't care about us,
   as well as those who
   do.

10. False (Mark 2:15).
    Jesus put His
    teachings into
    practice. People
    did not expect the
    Son of God to eat
    freely with sinners
    but to seek out the
    righteous.

11. d) go the extra mile
    for our enemies and
    to show them much
    love (Luke 6:29)

12. False (Luke 6:37).
    God is everyone's
    ultimate Judge, and
    He knows each
    person's heart. The
    issue of forgiveness
    is for Him to decide.
    God will remember
    how we respond to
    other people when
    it is time for Him to
    reward us in heaven.

13. b) everyone. Jesus
    means *all* people,
    regardless of
    where they live,

and regardless of whether you like them or not.

15. c) love God with all your heart, soul, and mind (Matthew 22:37)

16. "Thou shalt have no other gods before me" (Exodus 20:3 KJV).

17. Yes. These teachings are the same, even though the words are different. God says He is the Lord and we should not love any other god more than we love Him. Today that includes modern idols such as celebrities and things money can buy. Anything, including television, sports, and video games, can become an idol when it takes up too much of our time, thoughts, and energy—and takes us away from God.

18. b) love one another (John 13:34–35)

19. Judas Iscariot

20. c) thirty pieces of silver (Matthew 26:15). Note: Thirty pieces of silver were worth about 120 denarii, or four months' wages in the first century.

21. a) "Friend, wherefore art thou come?" (Matthew 26:50). Even in His time of betrayal, Jesus still addressed Judas as "Friend." This shows how Jesus followed his own difficult teachings regarding enemies.

24. All in a Day's Work

1. A parable is a story that teaches a lesson.

2. a) those who didn't love God wouldn't understand His teachings (Matthew 13:11–13)

3. False (Matthew 13:36)

4. False. None of the parables appears in the Gospel of John.

6. d) the head of a house. Note: The New International Version substitutes the word *landowner* for "householder."

7. c) the kingdom of heaven (Matthew 20:1)

8. Either a penny (KJV) or a denarius (NIV) is correct. Both translations refer to the same coin, which was a day's wages for a laborer at the time (Matthew 20:2).

9. d) all of the above

10. True (Matthew 20:3–6). He hired more in the third, sixth, ninth, and eleventh hours.

12. c) no one had hired them (Matthew 20:7)

13. c) "You also go and work in my vineyard" (Matthew 20:4, 7).

14. False (Matthew 20:9)

15. True (Matthew 20:8)

16. Yes (Matthew 20:11–12)

17. a) to take their pay and go, since they were paid what they were promised (Matthew 20:14)

18. True

20. d) those who are last on earth are first in heaven (Matthew 20:16)

21. d) all of the above. God is all powerful and in control of everything. He may do as He wishes, for He created heaven and earth. As the householder continued to look for laborers throughout the day, God looks for new people to follow Him throughout time. His door is always open to those who love Him, repent of their sins, and accept Jesus Christ as their Savior.

22. Sometimes God's ways do not seem fair to us. We might be jealous that some Christians seem to have more privileges, possessions, or better grades than we do. However, God is generous to us, too. Think about all that God has done for you.

25. Jesus Heals the Sick

1. a) the Gospels

3. False (Matthew 8:1–4). He told the man not to tell anyone, but to go directly to the priest and offer the sacrifice required under Moses' law.

4. d) giving an order for him to be healed (Matthew 8:5–13; Luke 7:1–10). Jesus healed the officer's servant merely by ordering him to get well. This was unusual because Jesus did not even enter the officer's house to see or touch the servant.

6. Jesus healed Peter's mother-in-law (Matthew 8:14–15). Peter is called Simon in Mark 1:30–31 and Luke 4:38–39, which also give accounts of this particular healing.

7. b) touching her hand (Matthew 8:14–15; Mark 1:30–31; Luke 4:38–39)

9. True (Luke 4:41)

10. False (Luke 4:41). Jesus gave the demons an order not to speak because He did not want them to tell who He was.

11. a) herd of pigs (Matthew 8:28–34; Mark 5:1–20; Luke 8:26–39)

12. b) were afraid (Mark 5:15; Luke 8:35)

13. True (Matthew 8:34; Mark 5:17; Luke 8:37)

14. After the man was healed, he wanted to go with Jesus (Mark 5:18; Luke 8:38).

15. True (Mark 5:19; Luke 8:39)

16. Yes (Mark 5:20)

17. a) clothing (Matthew 9:20; Mark 5:28; Luke 8:44)

18. d) faith (Matthew 9:22, Mark 5:34, Luke 8:48)

20. True (Matthew 9:23). In fact, preparations were already being made for her funeral.

21. sleeping (Matthew 9:24; Mark 5:39; Luke 8:52)

22. b) two blind men (Matthew 9:27–29)

26. The Lord's Prayer

2. The Lord's Prayer appears in both Luke and Matthew. The version from Matthew 6:9–13 is quoted here from the King James Version because it is the more complete of the two:

Our Father which art in heaven, Hallowed be thy name. Thy kingdom come, Thy will be done in earth, as it is in heaven. Give us this day our daily bread. And forgive us our debts, as we forgive our debtors. And lead us not into temptation, but deliver us from evil: For thine is the kingdom, and the power, and the glory, for ever. Amen.

3. a) one of them had asked him to teach them how to pray (Luke 11:1)

4. God is in heaven.

5. He means that we should respect, honor, and revere God's holy name.

7. True

8. True (Matthew 6:5)

9. A hypocrite is a person who acts like someone good in public but does evil things when no one else is watching.

10. False. The Lord's Prayer is a model for us to go by. However, sharing our own concerns with God helps us to become closer to Him. God loves you and He wants to hear

about your cares. He also likes for you to thank Him for his goodness.

12. This prayer is named the "Lord's Prayer" because Jesus taught it to us.

13. d) God will forgive us when we forgive others (Matthew 6:14–15)

27. The Ultimate Sacrifice

1. a) the kingdom of heaven (Matthew 5:10)

2. the Sermon on the Mount

3. a) Beatitudes (Matthew 5:3–12)

4. False (Matthew 5:10). People can be persecuted for many reasons, but it is those who are tormented for being Christians who will inherit the kingdom of heaven.

5. the prophets (Matthew 5:12)

6. the book of Acts

7. b) New Testament, following the Gospel of John. Note: This makes sense since the events described in Acts take place soon after Jesus' resurrection.

8. False (Acts 6:8)

9. Blasphemy is taking the Lord's name in vain. This violates the first of the Ten Commandments. When we take the Lord's name in vain, that means we are using it

disrespectfully and thoughtlessly. When we use the Lord's name, it should be during worship services, to praise Him or to speak to Him in prayer.

11. a) blasphemy (Acts 6:11). Because the Jewish people revere the Old Testament patriarchs (such as Moses and Abraham), using their names in a disrespectful manner was considered blasphemous.

12. False (Acts 6:11). Stephen's enemies could not defeat his wisdom in open debate, so they convinced some men to lie about Stephen.

13. c) an angel (Acts 6:15)

14. d) by giving a speech in defense of Christianity (Acts 7:1–53)

15. False (Acts 7:51–53). Stephen was saying that Israel was not faithful to the Lord, even though they were His chosen people.

16. c) the glory of God and Jesus at God's right hand in heaven (Acts 7:56)

17. Because he told everyone what he saw (Acts 7:56).

18. a) angry (Acts 7:57–58)

19. True (Acts 7:60)

21. No (Acts 7:58)

22. c) putting Christians in prison (Acts 8:3)

23. True

28. Jesus' Resurrection

1. True. Although all four Gospels don't talk about everything that happened to Jesus, all do record His resurrection (see Matthew 28:1–15; Mark 16:1–11; Luke 24:1–12; John 20:1–18).

2. Matthew 28:1 names Mary Magdalene, Mary the mother of James, and Salome. There were other unnamed women. Luke 24:10 names Joanna.

3. a) an angel of the Lord (Matthew 28:2)

4. c) "Fear not, for Jesus has risen" (Matthew 28:5-6). Note: An earthquake had already happened when the angel rolled away the stone (Matthew 28:2).

5. False (Luke 24:11). They thought the women were telling idle tales.

6. Jesus' disciples Peter and John went to the grave. The King James Version refers to John as "the other disciple whom Jesus loved" (John 20:2–4).

7. True (John 20:11–18)

8. c) "Peace be unto you" (John 20:19)

29. Luke Tells Us about Jesus

1. Luke's Gospel is the third book in the New Testament.

3. The Acts of the Apostles is the fifth book in the New Testament.

4. True

5. The four Gospels are: Matthew, Mark, Luke, John.

6. True. You can read about them in the Gospels. Some of them are recorded in Luke 4:31–5:26 and 6:6–19.

7. a) tax collectors and outcasts (Luke 5:30). Some religious leaders in Jesus' day did not understand why the Messiah would spend time with tax collectors and outcasts. In Jesus' day, tax collectors often kept much of the tax money for themselves and were thought to be stealing from others.

8. True (Luke 6:1–5). Some Pharisees were upset with Jesus' disciples for picking wheat to eat on the Sabbath. Jesus told them King David had fed his hungry troops rather than stick to a strict religious rule. It was hard for the Pharisees to argue with Jesus about this, since King David was a hero. Jesus' point was that people are more important than following rules.

9. c) a man with a paralyzed hand (Luke 6:6–10). Although Jesus knew He was being watched by enemies who were hoping He would break the Jewish law about the Sabbath, Jesus healed the man anyway. Jesus said it was lawful to do good on the Sabbath. Again, this showed how Jesus

valued people more than rules.

10. False (Luke 6:11). Jesus' enemies were angry that he had broken the Jewish law.

11. a) follower

12. Jesus' disciples are named in Luke 6:13–16. They are:
Simon, whom He named Peter
Andrew, Simon's brother
James
John
Philip
Bartholomew
Matthew
Thomas
James, son of Alphaeus
Simon, who was called the Patriot (or the Zealot)
Judas, son of James
Judas Iscariot, who became the traitor.

13. Soon after He chose His disciples, Jesus preached the Sermon on the Mount, also known as the Beatitudes (Luke 6:20–26).

14. False. Jesus said we should love our enemies (Luke 6:27).

15. The Golden Rule says to do unto others as you would have them do unto you. This means you should treat everyone else the same way you would like them to treat you.

16. False (Luke 6:37–42). We should be careful about how we judge other people because God will judge us by the same standards we use for others.

17. a) washed His feet

with her tears (Luke 7:36–38)

18. d) said that Jesus shouldn't let a sinful woman touch Him (Luke 7:39)

19. True (Luke 7:47)

30. Luke Tells Us What Jesus Said

1. A parable is a lesson told in story form.

2. d) His disciples could understand them, but not everyone else (Luke 8:10). Jesus did not want to share His knowledge with everyone—only those who truly wanted to follow Him.

3. False. Jesus said that His family are those who hear and obey God (Luke 8:21). This does not mean we are not to love and honor our families, but that we are to be close to people who love the Lord, whether or not they are family members.

4. a) John the Baptist (Luke 9:7–9, 18, 20). John the Baptist was a cousin of Jesus whose ministry was legendary. Some people also thought that Jesus was Elijah or another prophet come back to life.

5. *Resurrected* means "brought back to life from the dead."

6. True (Luke 9:21–22)

8. d) Moses and Elijah (Luke 9:31). This was amazing because both Moses and Elijah had long been dead.

9. Jesus' visitors talked to Him about how He would soon fulfill God's plan for Him (Luke 9:31).

11. b) were afraid and told no one (Luke 9:36)

12. True (Luke 9:46)

13. Jesus said that the person who is the least important on earth is the most important person in heaven. This is an important teaching of Jesus because it is the opposite of what the world teaches, and it even goes against our own human nature. Rather than looking to be the most important person in the world, it is better for us to put Jesus first.

14. a) told him to stop (Luke 9:49). They were upset because he was not part of their group.

15. Jesus said, "Forbid him not; for he that is not against us is for us" (Luke 9:50 KJV). This means Jesus welcomes all who love Him, not just people who belong to a certain group.

17. False. The Samaritan village did not want Jesus to come through there because He was on His way to Jerusalem. James and John asked Jesus if He wanted them to command fire to come from heaven to destroy the village (Luke 9:54).

18. c) not to be unforgiving toward the citizens of the town. He said, "Ye know not what manner of spirit ye are of; for the Son of

man is not come to destroy men's lives, but to save them" (Luke 9:55–56 KJV). This means he told the disciples not to be so mean-spirited. Jesus wants to save us.

19. False. Jesus and the disciples went another way (Luke 9:56).

21. d) nothing (Luke 10:4)

31. The Prodigal Son

1. Jesus told the story of the prodigal son.

2. You can find the story of the prodigal son in Luke 15:11–32.

3. False

4. The word *prodigal* means "recklessly extravagant; lavish."

5. The wealthy man had two sons (Luke 15:11).

6. a) give him his share of his inheritance (Luke 15:12)

7. b) property that is passed on when someone dies

8. True (Luke 15:11–13)

9. c) wasted his money (Luke 15:13)

10. d) tending pigs (Luke 15:15)

11. False (Luke 15:20). The father ran to the son, hugged him, and kissed him.

12. d) a ring, a robe, and shoes (Luke 15:22)

13. True (Luke 15:23–24)

14. False. He begged the older brother to join the party (Luke 15:28).

15. d) was angry (Luke 15:28)

16. He was upset because he had not been rewarded with a party, even though he had been faithful and had never strayed from the father (Luke 15:29–30).

17. c) "Everything I have is yours and we are close" (Luke 15:31).

18. True (Luke 15:32). The father said the younger brother had been lost but was found. He had been dead, but was alive.

32. The Good Samaritan

1. You can find the story of the good Samaritan in Luke 10:25–37.

2. False. The parable of the Good Samaritan can be found only in Luke.

4. c) a story that teaches a lesson

5. d) "Who is my neighbor?" (Luke 10:29)

6. a) a lawyer (Luke 10:25)

7. c) had been beaten and robbed (Luke 10:30)

8. False (Luke 10:31–32)

9. The man was on his way from Jerusalem to Jericho (Luke 10:30).

10. The Samaritan stopped to help the injured man (Luke 10:33).

13. c) oil and wine (Luke 10:34)

14. True (Luke 10:35)

15. c) an inn (Luke 10:34)

33. Martha

2. d) the Gospels of
   Luke and John (Luke
   10:38–41; John 11:1–
   44, 12:2)

3. Bethany (John 11:1)

4. True (John 11:3)

5. a) had perfumed Jesus'
   feet and wiped them
   with her hair (John
   11:2)

6. b) knew the sickness
   would be to God's
   glory (John 11:4)

7. False (John 11:6). He
   did not leave where
   he was for two days.

8. b) dead (John 11:17)

9. a) ran out to greet Him
   (John 11:20)

10. d) stayed in the house
    (John 11:20)

11. True (John 11:21)

12. True (John 11:24)

14. c) ran out to meet
    Jesus without delay
    (John 11:29)

15. They had not yet seen
    Jesus (John 11:30).
    In her eagerness to
    greet him, Martha
    had met Jesus
    outside of town. He
    had not yet arrived in
    town when Mary left
    the house.

16. True (John 11:32)

18. He wept because he
    was sad that Lazarus
    had died.

20. d) a cave, with a
    stone rolled over the
    entrance (John 11:38)

21. a) "Lord, by this time

he stinketh: for he
hath been dead four
days." (John 11:39)

22. True (John 11:40)

23. Yes (John 11:44)

24. Yes (John 12:2–3)

25. a) could have been
given to the poor
(John 12:5)

26. a) he was taking
money from the
disciples' funds for
himself (John 12:6)

27. Judas's betrayal of
Jesus should come
as no surprise since
he was dishonest all
along.

29. True (Luke 10:38)

30. c) asked Jesus to tell
Mary to help her
(Luke 10:40)

31. She was listening to
Jesus (Luke 10:39).

32. d) she should allow
Mary to listen to His
Word (Luke 10:41–42).

33. b) there is a time to
worry about physical
needs and a time to
listen to God

34. Paul Speaks about Love

1. The apostle Paul wrote
1 Corinthians.

2. b) members of the
church at Corinth.
Paul's letters to them
gave advice on how
they should live as
Christians.

4. False. Without love,
any speech is just
a lot of noise
(1 Corinthians 13:1).

5. d) none of the above.
You must have love
(1 Corinthians 13:2–3).

6. d) proud (1 Corinthians 13:4). This means you will let the person you love be first, or the most important.

7. This means if you love someone, it will take a lot to make you mad at that person.

8. False (1 Corinthians 13:8–9)

9. Love is the greatest (1 Corinthians 13:13).

35. The Fruit of the Spirit

1. c) a set of attitudes you'll have if you love God.

2. We can learn about the fruit of the Spirit in Galatians 5:22–23.

3. The apostle Paul told us about the fruit of the Spirit.

4. a) members of a group of churches in Galatia.

6. Paul speaks of love in 1 Corinthians 13.

7. b) happiness in the Lord.

9. c) you can forgive other people when they sin against you.

11. True (Galatians 5:22)

12. False. No matter what, a person of faith always believes in God (Hebrews 11:1).

13) c. strong, but kind to others

14. d) controlling yourself and not going to the extreme

15. False (Galatians 5:18). He wanted to show that Christian conduct is more

important than
following the law.

16. d) don't think about
their bodies as much
as they think about
living for Christ
(Galatians 5:25)

17. a) we obey Christ
(Galatians 5:25)

18. False. Christians
should not seek
others' possessions
(Galatians 5:26).

19. There are many
good reasons to
obey Christ. In this
passage, Paul is
showing us how
we will act if we are
obedient. Loving
others is a good way
to be an ambassador
for Christ.

20. The nine elements
of the fruit of the
Spirit are love,
joy, peace, long-
suffering, gentleness,

goodness, faith,
meekness, and
temperance.

36. 1 Peter

1. a) Peter

2. True

3. b) is named first in
every list of the
apostles in the Bible.
These lists are found
in Matthew 10:2–4;
Mark 3:13–19; Luke
6:12–16; and Acts
1:13–14.

4. b) persecuted
Christians (1 Peter 1:1)

5. d) eternal life. The
Christian looks
forward to living with
God in heaven rather
than having lots of
things here.

6. True (1 Peter 1:14).
Jesus' teachings go
against the world's

system of greed and materialism. Instead of encouraging us to get more stuff, he tells us God will provide our needs. When we trust God, there is no need to be greedy or to wish we had more than someone else.

7. *Redeemed* means "saved." Those who accept Jesus' gift of salvation are saved and forgiven for their sins.

8. a) Jesus (1 Peter 1:7–9). Jesus redeemed us when He was crucified on the cross.

9. "Thou shalt not covet" (Exodus 20:17). We should not be jealous of other people's things or accomplishments but be happy for them in their success. When you are jealous of someone, think about everything God has done for you.

10. The warning to put aside evil speaking might remind us of the commandment not to bear false witness (not to tell lies) against our neighbor (Exodus 20:16).

11. a) newborn babes (1 Peter 2:2). This means we should desire the pure milk of the word, which is the word of God.

12. d) make Christians grow (1 Peter 2:2). The more we read the Bible, the more we learn about Jesus and the Christian faith.

13. c) living stones (1 Peter 2:5)

14. True (1 Peter 2:5)

16. True (1 Peter 2:7). This means Jesus is the foundation of our faith.

17. This means people who don't want to obey Jesus will trip over His word and find it insulting and offensive.

18. True (1 Peter 2:11–12). We are ambassadors for Christ. Our conduct should cause unbelievers to praise the Lord.

19. A sojourner is a guest. We are guests in this world, because our true home is in heaven with the Lord. We can enjoy God's awesome creation while we live here.

20. False (1 Peter 2:11).

He means Christians are not at home in this world.

21. b) obey the laws of their nations (1 Peter 2:13). If we obey the law, no one can say we think we are above the law. Christians are obligated to be good citizens.

22. False (1 Peter 2:18). We are to forgive others.

23. a) remember how Jesus trusted God (1 Peter 2:23–24). Jesus did not insult people who insulted Him. He trusted God.

24. c) lost sheep (1 Peter 2:25). This means they were sinners who had gotten away from God.

25. The three parables are about the lost sheep (Matthew 18:12–14 and Luke 15:3–7); the lost son (Luke 15:11–32); and the lost coin (Luke 15:8–10).

26. Psalm 23 refers to Jesus as a shepherd.

27. *Submit* means "to comply, to obey, or to go along with someone."

28. False (1 Peter 3:1). The wife should submit to her husband, even if he does not obey Christ. This does not mean the wife is a slave to the husband or that she should be mistreated, but that she should honor her marriage vows. Because the Christian church was just beginning to take hold in the world at the time Peter wrote this letter, some women who proclaimed Christ were already married to men who practiced pagan religions. By giving this instruction, Peter was discouraging these women from divorce.

30. False (1 Peter 3:3–4). Beauty from within is precious to God.

31. d) honor their wives (1 Peter 3:7)

32. a) not as strong physically as her husband (1 Peter 3:7). This does not mean the woman is not as good as the man or inferior to him; it just means that she is not as muscular or as strong in the body. He was encouraging

husbands to look out for their wives' best interests and to protect them.

33. True (1 Peter 3:7)

34. True (1 Peter 3:14). Peter wrote this to encourage Christians who were suffering just for being Christians. Some important people in the government did not like Christians, and they tried to make their lives difficult. Sometimes people were even killed for being Christians.

35. b) meekness (1 Peter 3:15–16)

36. The Sermon on the Mount, where He preached the Beatitudes (Matthew 5:1–12; Luke 6:20–26).

38. d) when you love people, you can forget about their sins (1 Peter 4:8). It is easier to forgive someone you love than someone you hate.

39. True (1 Peter 4:15)

40. a) be busybodies

41. Our earthly shepherds in the church today are elders of the church, or pastors (1 Peter 5:1).

42. b) elders (1 Peter 5:5)

43. God wants us to respect our parents. They can teach us a lot about life and how to be Christians.

44. The devil is the enemy of Christians (1 Peter 5:8).

45. "Amen" is the last word in 1 Peter (1 Peter 5:14 KJV).

NOTES

NOTES

NOTES

NOTES

NOTES

NOTES